Printed in the United States of America
First Orman Press Printing: July 1996

ISBN: 0-9652262-0-4
Library of Congress Catalog Card Number: 96-092249

*This book is dedicated to my wife of 35 years,
Dr. Sadie McCalep, who has borne the heat of the pastorate
with me for the past 16 years. I thank God for her and her exceptional
gift of public relations. I am most appreciative for her sensitivity
to the church growth assimilation process. On countless occasions she
has helped new church members become secure family members, and has
assumed many significant ministry roles/tasks, only to later
relinquish the ministry into the confidence of others. I am
sincerely grateful for her love and her gifts of long-suffering,
forgiveness, and reconciliation.*

ACKNOWLEDGMENTS

I would first like to thank God for planting me in a vineyard where He was growing His church, and for gracing me with the spiritual gift of discernment that directed me to continuously attempt to seek, follow, and join Him at every point of the journey. I would like to thank the Greenforest Baptist Church family and its leadership for their submissiveness to the constant needs for change, and their willingness to allow me to lead (not muzzling the ox), and their obedience to plant and water in faith; behaving as if and knowing that God will give the increase. Further, I would like to thank Gloria Lightfoot, my executive assistant and administrative secretary for her loyalty throughout the journey and for her diligence in typing, ordering and reordering the manuscript. I am appreciative to Dr. Karlene Crawford, Minister of Christian Education at Greenforest, for her gift of systematic theology that she graciously utilized in the editing of the content, as well as for her critical thinking and general editing of the manuscript. I am most thankful to the Reverend Dr. J. Alfred Smith, Sr. for writing the *Foreword*, and also to all the contributing readers and others who read the manuscript and provided me with valuable feedback. Special thanks to Atty. Xavier Dicks of Farry Bell Press for sharing his knowledge and talents of publishing. Additionally, I would like to acknowledge Ernestine Hardge for her technical editing support and Connie Sandidge for her expert editing assistance, both of Greenforest.

FOREWORD

I have carefully read and studied the majority of the literature on church growth. In my seminary studies, my professors required me to read the literature of the best writers on church growth. This practice continued even into my days as a graduate student working for an earned doctorate. After completing my graduate studies, and after seeing the Allen Temple Baptist Church of Oakland, California grow into a mega church, under the leadership as Senior Pastor, assisted by Co-Pastor J. Alfred Smith, Junior, I decided to continue my studies on church growth, by studying at The School for Church Growth that was affiliated with Fuller Theological Seminary in Pasadena, California.

After being exposed to books and lectures by highly respected and recognized academics, who earn their livelihood as experts on church growth strategies, I still felt that I needed to listen and learn from a pastor-scholar, who could address the issues not only from a scholarly point of view, but who could enter emotionally into my perplexity, pain, and plight, and address the cultural peculiarities of growing an African-American church that was, ad Dr. Jeremiah Wright would say: *"Totally Christian, but unashamedly Black."* I found someone who knows me, who understands me and my plight, but who also is equally at home in academia. This person is Dr. George O. McCalep, Jr., Pastor of Greenforest Baptist Church of Decatur, Georgia.

I was not just satisfied to hear Dr. George McCalep lecture, because I have heard many pastors who could speak well, but who had not even built "a chicken coop," so I decided to visit Greenforest Baptist Church to see if Dr. McCalep was simply "rapping without mapping." When my wife and I and a delegation from Allen Temple Baptist Church visited Greenforest, we concluded that the church was indeed a Greenforest led by an humble, but creative and brilliant pastor, who had not allowed phenomenal success go to his head. His ministry is also enriched by the able assistance of Mrs. McCalep and very loyal and gifted persons on the pastoral staff. I am happy that I was one of the many persons who encouraged Dr. McCalep to put his story in writing in this excellent manuscript, *Faithful Over a Few Things.*

Persons who read this book will fall deeply in love with one of the seven chapters, although each page of the book is priceless and precious. However, the portion that completely won me over to us-

viii

ing this book as a text in my seminary teaching, is the section on "Praying in Faith." No where had I seen this peculiar emphasis, unless it was when I was lecturing and preaching in Korea or was visiting with Dr. Harold Carter of the New Shiloh Baptist Church of Baltimore. Dr. McCalep writes in great depth about the interrelatedness of expressive praise and praying in faith.

As both a professor at the American Baptist Seminary of The West and the Graduate Theological Union in Berkeley, California, and as the Senior Pastor of Allen Temple Baptist Church of Oakland, California, I can truthfully say that no author and no book on church growth strategies have informed and inspired me like Dr. George McCalep and his book, *Faithful Over a Few Things.*

This book will become the 1997 study book of the Allen Temple Baptist Church and the required text for all of my seminary students in church administration. Do not delay in securing your copy of this book.

- **Dr. J. Alfred Smith, Sr.**
Professor, American Baptist Seminary of the West
and the Graduate Theological Union, Berkeley, California
Senior Pastor, Allen Temple Baptist Church, Oakland, California
Past President, Progressive National Baptist Convention, Inc.

TABLE OF CONTENTS

Prologue

A Call to Become Time Focused

"His lord said unto him, Well done, good and faithful servant; thou hast been faithful over a few things, I will make thee ruler over many things: enter thou into the joy of thy lord" (Matthew 25:21).

This book is based on three assumptions: (1) the pastor is the chief catalyst in church growth; (2) there is but so much time in a day, therefore, what the pastor can do is limited; and (3) if the church and her leadership do a few things well, God will grow His church. This book is designed not only for pastors, but also for supporting leadership. This information is offered so that the church as a body can be more aware of and sensitive to what absolutely must not be ignored or relegated to second place, so the church can grow. Although this book is concerned with time management, the major emphasis is on time focus. It is an attempt to help busy pastors and other church leaders stay focused on those things that have repeatedly proven to be the most essential components for church growth. This book is designed to be read over and over again so that these few church growth absolutes can be indelibly ingrained into the church's lifestyle for church growth.

This book is not culturally specific. Nor is it designed, focused, or oriented specifically toward any particular denomination. The only specific is church growth. This book is designed for churches that are interested in church growth, both numerically and spiritually. This book is strictly unapologetic for numerical growth. As a matter of fact, I believe the lack of numerical growth is due to the lack of spiritual growth. The two are not incompatible. Spiritual growth is a precursor to numerical growth. This book is not a theology book, although the principles set forth are biblical and scripturally referenced. This book is pragmatic in that the "how to do it" is never neglected. I am a practitioner of church growth. Even as of the writing of this book, the principles set forth in the book are being actualized at the church I pastor. The seven principles set forth in this book have led Greenforest to grow from a declining church of 25 members to a growing church of over 4000 active members in the last 16 years. There are only a few church growth consultants with a successful track record who are actively pastoring.

The language of the book may be persuasive and oftentimes may seem "preachy." This is simply the result of my burden for all churches to grow. God has placed a calling on me that extends beyond the church I pastor. I feel that I am a man on a mission to help other churches grow. God has gifted and prepared and burdened me for the journey. The brevity of the book is intentional. Prayerfully it will lend itself to this pragmatic endeavor. This book is designed to help you "do it." Read it and do it (the few things) and God's church will grow.

Again, the book is about a few things that a church and her leadership must do to fulfill God's purpose for church growth. Notice I mention it is God's purpose for churches to grow. The Great Commission of Matthew clearly gives us this mandate. I have been blessed over the past 16 years to pastor a growing church; therefore, I am constantly called upon to preach and lecture at numerous church growth and evangelism conferences. I have been afforded the opportunity to study with and listen to the best in the field. These opportunities have motivated me to read a vast number of books written about church growth. I have been motivated and driven to read, study, and analyze church growth literature. Also, I have been forced to analyze my personal experiences, leadership style, events, and methods that have led to the considerable growth that has taken place at the church God called me to pastor. When asked to tell the "Greenforest Miracle Growth Story," it has not been enough to simply say, "God did it" even though, indeed, He did do it! But my colleagues and audiences have asked, "How did God do it?", "What did you do to get it done?", "What did you do so God could work through you?", "What are the causative factors and principles?" My findings were many. Much has been written about methods, marketing techniques, and principles. Characteristics related to growing churches have been identified. My thinking was that what the church needed least was one more book on church growth. In my own pursuit to prioritize my time in maintaining a growing church, God kept speaking to me saying, "If you are faithful over a few things...", thus the inspiration for writing this book. We do not have to try everything or try every method. But if we are faithful over a few things, seven things to be exact, He will bless us in our church growth efforts. This book is truly about putting first things first relative to Kingdom building.

> Jesus said, "But seek ye first the kingdom of God, and his righteousness; and all these things shall be added unto you" (Matt. 6:33).

This book is about putting God first in the Kingdom building process. I have tried to condense the "few things" into seven principles. Why seven? First, I have learned that seven is a perfect number in the Hebrew language. Secondly, and not necessarily in prioritized ranking, I learned in behavioral science that any listing of do's, don'ts, guidelines, etc. that exceed seven is counterproductive. Mainly, seven is the greatest number of balls that I can juggle or saucers I can spin at one time. One of the greatest inspirations of my pastorate came while in a frustrated state of trying to manage time. I saw myself as a man in the circus or carnival trying to keep the saucers spinning on seven poles. When I had the seventh (last) saucer spinning, the first one fell off the pole. Nothing really happens in the church unless the pastor gives it his attention. Just about the time the Sunday School, praise worship service, and discipleship training saucers are spinning, etc., the first saucer falls. Then at a certain point they all fall. Sometimes the anxiety is so great when they all fall, that it is difficult to get anything started again. Can you see yourself in this illustration? Thank God He told me, "If I can be faithful over a few things...". The few things are presented and discussed in the seven chapters.

As one is aware, there are many other things that are important to the life of the church and the role of the pastor, such as pastoral counseling, political involvement, committee meetings, board assignments, leadership training, supervising paid staff, problem solving, decision making, conflict management, denominational service, visiting the sick, community involvement, building projects, performing weddings, officiating funerals and others. If you do the seven suggested things well, many of these other things will take care of themselves. It is not my suggestion that these other things are trivial. Some may be important—others may actually be counterproductive to church growth. They certainly are time consuming. Again, one of the basic tenets of this book is that there is but so much time in a day. The pastor is the catalyst for church growth, so he must prioritize how he is going to spend his time. He must decide what he can easily delegate and what he must carefully delegate. Effective leadership theory teaches us that a good leader delegates everything except those things that must be done by the leader. The seven few things suggested for church growth obviously cannot all be done by any one person. But they must be the leader's focus of attention. If the pastor and the church will do these few things well, the church will grow.

Chapter 1

Cherish and Prioritize Relationships

Churches that are faithful over the essential principles of church growth cherish and put relationships first. Building relationships should be the number one goal of the church.

The Importance of Relationships
Relationships are of the utmost importance. The word *relationship* is the most important word in church growth, second only to the word *gospel*. "Relationships have many characteristics of living things. They are born, and they can die. Relationships can be damaged, mended, broken, healed, diminished, built up, enhanced, cultivated, sought, improved, rejected, cheap when purchased, valuable when given away, young, old, fresh, stale, warm, cool, cold, conspicuous by absence, long-term, short-term, beautiful, ugly, cherished, taken for granted, special, ignored, time-consuming, time saving, beneficial, draining, blessings, or curses. Nearly everything we are about depends on the quality of relationships: our marriage and family, our friendships, our employment, and our very legitimacy as a person."[1]

Relationships are so important that they must be cherished. *Cherish* means to care for and to nurture. Cherishing relationships in the church is no different than cherishing relationships in a marriage. It does not just happen. You have to work at it. You must develop it. You must be committed to making it work. In spite of whatever happens, the relationship is so important that you will never walk away from it and never turn your back on it. It is absolutely necessary for the pastor and church leaders to be in a constant, visible, loving relationship. The greatest church tragedy today is the broken relationship, or perceived broken relationships, between pastor and deacons, elders, and other significant lay leaders. As I travel across this country and listen to the horror stories that come from church board rooms and business meetings, it is a wonder that these churches continue to exist. The sad commentary is that some think poor relationships between pastors and deacons are normal. When the pastor and church leadership are perceived to be separated, the church will be separated. On the other hand, if the pastor and the leadership are perceived to be together, the general congregation will be together. Church growth is much like playing winning basketball; togetherness is essential. The right chemistry must be on the team. Sometimes that means playing a lesser skilled player to provide the right chemistry to put a "W" in the win column.

Notice I said when it is *perceived* that the pastor and leaders are together or are not together. In church growth, relationship perception is particularly important. The reality is insignificant relative to the perception, or as we learn in management theory, perception is real to the person having the perception. The congregation must perceive the leadership to be bonded in a loving relationship. My experience teaches that there is no such thing as a church disagreement outside the ranks of the leadership. Leadership may claim that "they" feel disenchanted, but the "they" always begins at the level of the leadership. Therefore, for churches to grow the church and her leadership must perform as a marriage. This marriage must be developed and nurtured. The marriage must be cherished.

Five Stages in Relationship Development

The fact that relationships are developed indicates that there are stages in the development process. Jack Smith, for the purpose of relational evangelism identifies five stages that are applicable to any relationship development process: (1) the preexistent stage, (2) the first impression stage, (3) the acquaintance stage, (4) the maturing stage, and (5) the tried, tested and proven stage.[2] As alluded to earlier, we are all involved in relationships one way or another. Relationships cannot be avoided. At what stage are you and/or your church in your various relationships?

The church and the pastor are always in a pre-existent stage because of the identification labels. In other words, your reputation precedes you. You are known by many in a certain way. The key is, are you known as someone who cherishes relationships? Pastors of growing churches are often already known to care about people and the welfare of people. Of course the opposite may also be true.

The second stage is the first impression stage. The first impression stage can be positive or negative. Negative first impressions are difficult to correct. Once the jury has heard it, no overruling can wipe from their minds what the jury has already heard. How you dress, what you say, how you said it provide a blueprint for first impressions. A first impression often neglected by many churches is the cleanliness, landscaping and manicuring of the church facility. That is the first thing people see when they drive up to the church. Also, parking lot attendants, though well-meaning, are often task-oriented and not evangelistically trained volunteer personnel. They provide first impressions. It is suggested for ultimate growth, evangelistically trained persons be utilized as parking lot greeters. Clear signs directing people to various classes are important. In general, today's growth-oriented church must become user friendly. User-friendly strategies make for good first impressions.

The third stage is the acquaintance stage. The key to the acquaintance stage is knowing something about the other person, especially their name. Everybody wants to go where somebody knows his name. Some people believe the gift of remembering names and/or faces is given to some and not to others. However, I am reminded that the CIA trains people to remember faces and names. If relationships are cherished, the pastor and leadership will diligently and deliberately attempt to learn faces and names. Photos of new members can be posted as well as distributed and studied at staff meetings. Associated memory workshops can be instituted for staff. The acquaintance stage is a key stage in the church growth process. We can ill afford to be brothers and sisters in Christ and strangers in the pews. Even a portion of the worship service should be designed for more than a casual welcome. Is it not rewarding and comforting to know that in our relationship with God, God knows "the very hairs of our head?"

The fourth stage is the maturing relationship. Maturity is developed in relationships in the midst of a struggle, during the storms, during the heat of the journey, when disagreement is the state of affairs, and when conflict occurs. It may be said that every relationship is either entering the storm, in a storm, or on the way out of a storm. Storms do come. The scriptures promise us that we will have trials and tribulations. Christianity is not guaranteed to be trouble free. As a matter of fact, it promises persecution and adversity. "So that we ourselves glory in you in the churches of God for your patience and faith in all your persecutions and tribulations that ye endure: Which is a manifest token of the righteous judgment of God, that ye may be counted worthy of the kingdom of God, for which ye also suffer" (2 Thess. 1:4-5). Although the scripture promises that we will not be trouble free, we are also told that we should be anxiety free if we are in a loving covenant relationship with God. "And why take ye thought for raiment? Consider the lilies of the field, how they grow; they toil not, neither do they spin: And yet I say unto you, That even Solomon in all his glory was not arrayed like one of these. Therefore, if God so clothe the grass of the field, which to day is, and to morrow is cast into the oven, shall he not much more clothe you, O ye of little faith? Therefore take no thought, saying, What shall we eat? or, What shall we drink? or, Wherewithal shall we be clothed? (Matt 6:28-31). Truly, His eye is on the sparrow, so we know He watches over us.

The key components in maturing relationships are acceptance, appreciation, and dependence on God and each other. I may disagree with you, but I accept you. In spite of our differences, I appreciate you and I am depending on you. The maturing stage is the test period in the relationship building process.

The fifth stage is the tried, tested and proven stage. This the stage in the relationship when all the exit lights have been turned off. One of my pastoral marriage counseling procedures attempts to get couples who have domestic relationship problems to cut off all exit lights. In other words, make a deliberate decision based on a covenant relationship with God, and each other, to maintain the relationship. The mind set should be, that regardless of the circumstance and situation, the relationship will not be broken. That is what God does for us when he saves us. He has entered into a relationship with us that He promises to maintain for an eternity. Relationships that have come through storms and are proven, tried and tested must always depend on God.

The Need

The need for loving and supportive relationships is not only vast, but also increasing. Terry McMillan's novel, *Waiting to Exhale*, describes the desperate need for relationships in our society. The novel depicts the plight of four African-American women who cry together, suffer together, and party together as they wait on that right man to come along and take their breath away. They wait for Mr. Right or Mr. Wonderful to come into their lives. They are waiting for someone with whom they can trust their emotions, their deepest inner virtues, their love, the very essence of themselves. They are "waiting to exhale." They are waiting on that right relationship. I am reminded that Jesus met a Samaritan woman at Jacob's well who, likewise, had been in and out of several ill-planned relationships in that she had had five husbands and was currently involved with another man who was not her husband. Like the women in Terry McMillan's novel, she had experienced rejection and prejudice. Some spiritual dialogue with Jesus led to Jesus' confronting her sins, giving her the knowledge of who He was, and inviting her to experience a new relationship through the partaking of living water. Once she entered into a new relationship with Jesus, she dropped her water pots and ran to the village to tell the people, particularly the men, to come see a man who loved her in spite of her faults. This is the relationship for which the world hungers. Most of today's society is "waiting to exhale." Waiting on the right relationship. Waiting on a relationship rooted in Godly (agape) love.

Societal demands and pressures drive us to seek some permanence in our lives. We live in a mobile society. People are constantly moving from one city to another, from one job to another. We are constantly being separated from one thing or another. We are separated from our careers through layoffs and downsizing. We are often separated from our loved ones by death, divorce, crime, or violence. Deteriorating schools and declining family values all contribute to the need and desire for Godly permanent relationships. Corporate America is downsizing and divorce is at an all-time high. Psychologists tell us that divorce is second only to death as an anxiety producing factor. People come to church needing, seeking and wanting relationships. So what is the solution?

The solution is found in God. But where do we find God? God is found in a relationship. A relationship with God is manifested in a relationship with another child of God. We, the church, must do a better job of focusing our time and efforts on relationships. When we fail to cherish and prioritize relationships, the church becomes a part of the problem and not the solution..When the church gets out of focus and permits separation and feelings of rejection to exist in its ministries, then the church has become a mirror of society. Pastors and church leaders should make sure that they are faithful in attending to the need for relationships.

The problem we have in building relationships in the church is that the whole process stands in opposition to what the world and secular society teach. Society teaches the values of rugged individualism, independence, do your own thing, and have it your way. These agents work against the establishment of relationships where people are dependent on God and other people.

The Components

What are the key components of godly relationships? Simply, they are people, love, bonding, and family. Our definition of a godly relationship is two or more people connected together (bonded) as brother and sister (family) by the power of God's love.

People. The first component in relationships is people. Simply put, people matter. People are important. Why are people so important? Because people are God's crowned creation. God declared it when the psalmist asked: "What is man, that thou art mindful of him? And the son of man, that thou visitest him? For thou hast made him a little lower than the angels, and hast crowned him with glory and honour. Thou madest him to have dominion over the works of thy hands; thou hast put all things under his feet:" (Ps 8:4-6).

What is man? According to God, man is His crowned creation. People are important to God. People are more important to God than people are to people. God thinks more about man than man thinks of himself. Man's theories of who he is have fallen short of God's glory. The evolutionist, Charles Darwin, reported man as a creature evolved from lower animals. Carl Marx might say that man is but an economic factor. Sigmund Freud would say that man is but an instinct. But when God was asked the question, "What is Man?" God refers to man as His crowned and honored creation. Understanding the fact that God would be so mindful of man led the psalmist to open and close the eighth Psalm by exclaiming, "O LORD our Lord, how excellent is thy name in all the earth!" Not only were we made a little lower than the angels and crowned with His glory, verse six tells us, "Thou madest him to have dominion over the works of thy hands; thou hast put all things under his feet:" (Ps 8:6).

God has made us stewards over all things, including ourselves. The church must possess a stewardship of people. We must minister to people. People are God's glory and honor. It must never be forgotten that people are our primary concern, not programs, plans and buildings. The church is not a building. Rather, the church is a called out people. Moses forgot that people were important to God. He got mad and frustrated with the murmurings of God's people while leading them out of bondage. Moses was denied initial entrance into the promised land because of his forgetfulness. God's people may be weak, but they are still God's people. They may sometimes act self-ish and uncommitted, but they are still God's people. Pastors and other church leaders must realize that they must cherish relation-ships with God's people because God's people are God's crowned and honored creation.

Love and Bonding. Love is the essential component in relationships. No method, procedure, program or process has any value unless love is present. God makes clear to us in the thirteenth chapter of 1 Corinthians, that without love everything else is futile.

> "Though I speak with the tongues of men and of angels, and have not charity, I am become as sounding brass, or a tinkling cymbal. And though I have the gift of prophecy, and understand all mysteries, and all knowledge; and though I have all faith, so that I could remove mountains, and have not charity, I am nothing. And though I bestow all my goods to feed the poor, and though I give my body to be burned, and have not charity, it profiteth me nothing. Charity suffereth long, and is kind; charity envieth not; char-ity vaunteth not itself, is not puffed up, Doth not behave itself unseemly, seeketh not her own, is not easily provoked, thinketh no evil; Rejoiceth not in iniquity, but rejoiceth in the truth; Beareth all things, believeth all things, hopeth all things, endureth all things. Charity never faileth: but whether there be prophecies, they shall fail; whether there be tongues, they shall cease; whether there be knowledge, it shall vanish away. For we know in part, and we proph-esy in part. But when that which is perfect is come, then that which is in part shall be done away. When I was a child, I spake as a child, I understood as a child, I thought as a child: but when I became a man, I put away childish things. For now we see through a glass, darkly; but then face to face: now I know in part; but then shall I know even as also I am known. And now abideth faith, hope, charity, these three; but the greatest of these is charity" (1 Cor. 13).

When I read 1 Corinthians 13, I am reminded of a basketball tournament where many teams begin the tournament, only to get eliminated in the first several rounds. Only faith, hope and love (the final three) made it to the last round. Notice the gift of speaking in tongues was eliminated in an earlier round; "Though I speak with the tongues of men and of angels, and have not charity, I am become as sounding brass, or a tinkling cymbal". (vs 1). Also, the gift of prophesy; "And though I have the gift of prophecy,... and have not charity, I am nothing". (vs 2). And the gift of benevolence; "And though I bestow all my goods to feed the poor,... and have not charity, it profiteth me nothing.", (vs 3). Only hope, faith and love survived early elimination.

Earlier in my life, it bothered me that hope and faith could ever be eliminated. However, through the power of the Holy Spirit, I realized that we will not need faith or hope when we stand before the One we hope to see. Only love remains forever, for God is love. Paul tells us that nothing can separate us from God's love. It is God's love that connects us in relationships.

Both love and bonding play a major role in godly relationships. Colossians tells us that love is the "perfect bond of unity" (Col. 3:14 NAS). This is not pretend love. This is godly love. God is many things, but He is not the great pretender. God is real and His love is real. Jesus constantly prays for a right relationship between his disciples, and between Him and His disciples that, "they may be one, just as We are one; I in thee, and Thou in Me, that they may be perfected in unity" (John 17:22-23 NAS). We are talking about relationships held together by love. Paul speaks of this love in Romans 8:35. "Who shall separate us from the love of Christ?" The love of Christ holds us together. The Greek translation for *hold* is *sunecho*, which means "pressed together". Love presses us one to another like Super Glue. Elmer Towns elaborates on this bonding process.

> The old term is to "join" a church, or to be "assimilated" into a church fellowship. These terms were adequate when the average American was loyal to the institutions in his community. The new term is "bonding." When a person is bonded to a contemporary church, the process is similar to that when using Super Glue.

> The old name for an adhesive was "paste" or "mucilage." It was just a gum or glue that stuck two things together. In the same way, church membership in the old days was the adhesive that held the member to the church, because it specified what a member must believe and how a member must behave.

Super Glue is not an adhesive. It does not *paste* two elements together, but *bonds* them, by absorbing itself into the elements of the two surfaces so that the two actually fuse or melt into one. In the old days, paste would break and things would separate. But when you secure two pieces of wood together with Super Glue, the wood will splinter before the Super Glue will break because the two are bonded into one. [3]

Bonding cannot be forced, and neither should it be delayed. The earlier the bonding process begins after new members join, the higher the probability that it will occur. According to Elmer Towns,

Bonding is similar to the process of 'imprinting'—an act in the natural world whereby a newborn animal attaches itself, in a sense of belonging, to an agent that is responsive to it immediately after birth or hatching. An example of imprinting is shown in a famous picture of the Nobel Prize winning naturalist Konrad Lorenz showing him being followed by a group of ducklings. The ducklings had attached themselves to him as their protective parent.

As with ducklings, bonding produces a relationship that can withstand separations. The ducklings followed Lorenz everywhere and did not unlearn the relationship during periods of separation. It is as though God has placed in the newborn a divinely-engineered factor, whether psychological or physiological, that prepares them for bonding to a parent.[4]

Family. Another component of relationships is the whole concept of family or kinship. Traditional churches talk about becoming a member of the church. Growth-oriented churches speak in terms of bonding with a family. Growth-oriented churches think and behave as an extended family. In many cases, unfortunately, the church is a member's only family. Family is desirable because relationships are desirable. What is family? According to Webster's dictionary, there is room for various definitions. Family is (1) a group of individuals living under one roof and usually under one head, (2) the basic unit in society having as its nucleus two or more adults living together and cooperating in the care and rearing of their own or adopted children,

(3) a group of persons of common ancestry (4) a large group of related plants or animals, and (5) a group of things related by common characteristics.

The key word in the definition of family seems to be "related." This is why family is such a key component of relationships. My working definition for family is "one or more persons birthed into a relationship, who live under some authority that transforms their character and shapes their outcome." The church family conforms to this definition. Church members are birthed into the family of God by adoption. We are birthed into a parenting and brother/sister relationship: "To redeem them that were under the law, that we might receive the adoption of sons. And because ye are sons, God hath sent forth the Spirit of his Son into your hearts, crying, Abba, Father" (Gal 4:5,6). We are further related because we live under the authority of Christian precepts that are from God and recorded in His word. That word transforms who we are and ultimately determines our destination.

The characteristics of the extended church family are much the same as any other family. First, there must be a parenting relationship in any family. The pastor, with his many roles, must not yield to the temptation of being an aloof dictatorial ruler, but maintain some perceivable image of parent. Parenting must take place beyond the level of the pastor. One-on-one discipleship is a good option. Modeling is inevitable. Children model parental behavior. Second, discipline is a needed factor in any family relationship. Like any well ordered family, discipline must be done in love and according to scriptural teaching. Third, forgiveness must be the basic governing staple in a family relationship. Saints do sin. God is faithful to forgive and so should we. A child should always be able to come home. Fourth, the family should be a place where family members feel secure and protected. The arms of a parent have always been a place of refuge for a child. Fifth, time must be treated as an investment for a family to be healthy. Busy pastors and church leaders must give prime time to cherishing church family relationships. Not just time, but as in any other family, quality time is the key. Sixth, diversity is a major characteristic of any family. However, diversity does not mean chaos. We can agree to disagree. We can agree to be agreeable even when we disagree. Diversity gives strength to the family when acceptance and appreciation for the worth and dignity of each family member are emphasized. Unity can be maintained in diversity. Seventh, family teaches and promotes values. The old adage is true, "If you do not stand for something, you will fall for anything." Family teaches family members what the standards are. The family serves as a plumb line that verbalizes and models what ought to be.

The Problem

The concept of family is both biblical and theological; however, it is often not practiced in the local church. Paul's letter to the Ephesians is replete with references to the church as body and as family. The first half of chapter two talks about the glorious work of salvation by grace through faith. The last half of the chapter deals with the results of salvation, that is, the workmanship of God. Paul alludes to the uniting of Jews and Gentiles, two separate and alienated groups of persons, into one new person (see vv. 13-15). The imagery reminds us of the miracle of marriage where two persons become one flesh. Paul follows this discussion with three illustrations for the new community which has been founded in Christ. The first is citizenship, the second is family, and the third is a holy temple (see vv. 19-21). "We are fellow-citizens with one another: we are brothers and sisters in God's household, and we form a living temple for the indwelling presence of God's Spirit."[5]

The problem is three-fold. First those outside the church do not trust the church. They enter the church with an untrusting behavior that must be overcome. Second, many in the secular world are prideful; they value their independence and self-sufficiency. Though their hearts yearn for true community and relationships, their intellectual minds want to stay independent. The result is a secular/spiritual schizophrenic monster. Third, many unchurched or once church-going believers have been hurt by a previous dysfunctional church family. They may have been abused by dictatorial pastor/parent rule or suffered through church meeting fights or been lulled into complacency by church apathy. They need family, but they are distrusting toward family because they have been hurt by family.

> This is made more complex first of all by the fact that the church is made up of persons who are at different stages of spiritual development. Some are spiritual preschoolers who need constant attention. Some are developing adolescents with their emotional highs and lows. Second, the church family receives new children by birth (evangelism) and by adoption (transfer). Some adopted children may come from dysfunctional church families and may have never experi-

enced healthy church relationships. Some may have been relationally abused by their former pastor-parent and thus have trouble relating to another pastor. The presence of adopted children or teenagers will always change family dynamics. Their healing and assimilation into the family requires the rest of the family to take time for consistently modeling healthy relationships.[6]

We must treat the unchurched gently if we are to win them and others back into the family of God. "Many churches are inclusive in outreach, yet exclusive in fellowship. People can be reached, baptized, and brought into membership and not be incorporated into the friendship (family) structure of the church."[7] The church and her leadership must be concerned not only with seeking and finding, but also keeping and nurturing. Bonding people together by love through family is the best way to accomplish this task.

Notice that the ten commandments put man either in a right relationship with God or a right relationship with man. The first four commandments deal with duties toward God and the last six concern human relationships.

1. I am the Lord thy God. Thou shalt have no other gods before me.
2. Thou shalt not make thee any graven image, or any likeness of any thing that is in heaven above, or that is in the earth beneath, or that is in the waters beneath the earth...
3. Thou shalt not take the name of the LORD thy God in vain...
4. Remember the Sabbath day, to keep it holy...
5. Honor thy father and thy mother.
6. Thou shalt not kill.
7. Thou shalt not commit adultery.
8. Thou shalt not steal.
9. Thou shalt not bear false witness against thy neighbor.
10. Thou shalt not covet thy neighbor's house, nor thy neighbor's wife, nor his manservant, nor his maidservant, nor his ox, nor his ass, nor any thing that is thy neighbor's.

Six Kinds of Relationships

Ken Hemphill identifies six kinds of relationships that must be cherished and prioritized for the church to flourish according to the will of God. These must be (1) a right relationship between the pastor and God; (2) a right relationship between the church members and God; (3) the right relationship between the pastor and the members, especially other church leaders; (4) the right relationship between the members and the pastor; (5) the right relationship among the members; and (6) the right relationship between the church and the world. Remember, church growth is a direct outcome of right relationships with God, and right relationships with God are manifested in right relationships among God's people.

Between Pastor and God. First, a right relationship between the pastor and God is absolutely necessary for godly church growth. One of the premises of this book is that the pastor is the catalyst for growth in the church. If the pastor is living in any way out of the will of God, church growth will suffer. For example, suppose the pastor is not a tither. Unfortunately, through inquiry I have found this example to be more typical than atypical. Tithing we know is more a matter of faith than money. Failure to tithe clearly puts a person outside the will of God. If the leader's faith in God is weak, the congregation's faith will be weak as well. Other examples, such as the pastor's not managing his home well or being a womanizer or living a double life can also inhibit church growth.

Between Members and God. The second key relationship is a right relationship between the members of the church and God. Often members interpret their role as spectators in the family of God. Being a bench or pew warmer is not the same as being in a right relationship with God. Members must be encouraged and given opportunities to become participants at every level of church activity. Every member should be a learner and follower of Christ. Therefore, the entire church family should be committed to discipleship training. All should have the lyric and melody of this old favorite hymn of the church in their hearts. "Just a closer walk with Thee, grant it, Jesus, if you please, daily walking close with Thee, let it be, dear Lord, let it be."

Between Pastor and Members. The third relationship that needs to be prioritized is a right relationship between the pastor and the members, especially other church leaders. I personally do not have any enemies in the church; maybe some confused friends, but definitely no enemies. I have never felt that I was gifted in the area of preaching, singing, etc., but I am thankful for the gift of love for the people. I often tell the congregation that if I can't preach the hell out of them, I am confident that I can love the hell out of them.

Between Members and Pastor. The fourth crucial relationship is between the members and the pastor. Most churches do not provide opportunities for this relationship to be strengthened. People *learn* to love, and they learn best in practice. The annual pastor's anniversary or pastor's appreciation day is an excellent way for the congregation to express love for the pastor. Like any worthwhile activity, this activity can be and has been abused and misused. However, when properly utilized it represents an excellent opportunity for the members to show their appreciation to the pastor. If there are monetary gifts to the pastor, they should not be part of a budget line item. This defeats the purpose. In addition, this should not be a time-consuming fund raiser, as that would also defeat the purpose. A day each year should be dedicated to the pastor and supported by the church and her leadership. A love offering could be lifted for the pastor. This is not a matter of paying the pastor, for no amount of money can pay for the blessing of having a loving effective pastor. The real purpose is to create an opportunity for the church and, more importantly, individual members to express their love to pastor.

Through the storms, trials and tribulations, it has been the expressions of love given by individual members, in many cases members I thought did not care, that have kept me encouraged. Thank God for the expressions of love that come when I need them most. Needless to say, many churches are opposed to a pastor's anniversary day because they cannot see beyond the money issue and the issue of honoring a human. Members can love their pastor without worshiping him and should be given an opportunity to demonstrate that love. A right relationship between the members and the pastor is of utmost importance if the church is to grow. Scripture teaches that "My sheep hear my voice, and I know them, and they follow me" (John 10:27). While it is true that the voice in this passage is Jesus' voice, it is also true that a right relationship with the pastor is needed so the undershepherd's voice will be heard.

Between Members and Members. The fifth right relationship needed for maximum church growth is the relationship between members.

The Bible says, "Beloved, let us love one another: for love is of God; and every one that loveth is born of God, and knoweth God" (I Jn 4:7). Charity begins at home, loving and taking care of each other. Most Christians do well taking care of one another in short-term crises such as when there is death in the family. But most fail miserably loving one another in good times. We are saddened when others are saddened, but we cannot rejoice when others rejoice. Also, we oftentimes fail miserably in cases of longsuffering such as divorces, terminal illnesses, especially illnesses outside our comfort zones such as AIDS.

Most feel freedom from hate automatically means love. This is not so. One can be free from hate and not demonstrate love. Love must be shown to be effective. We must teach people to obey the greatest commandment of all, and that is to love. We must remember the latter part of The Great Commission, "teaching them to obey everything I have commanded you" (Matt 28:20 NIV).

Between the Church and the World. The sixth and final right relationship that will result in church growth is the relationship between the church and missions or the world. Missions is defined as service to God and God's creation outside the four walls and stained glass windows of the church. Missions means giving yourself away to others. God promises a blessing to them who give to others. The Gospels declare, "For whosoever will save his life shall lose it: and whosoever will lose his life for my sake shall find it" (Matt 16:25, Mk 8:35, Lk 9:24). In other words if you spend your life, you save your life; if you lose your life, you gain your life. A right relationship with God calls us to reach out beyond ourselves to others. Missions is doing unto the "least of these my brethren" (Matt 25:40). Notice Jesus identifies with the poor, the least, and the unlikely. When we serve the least, we minister unto Jesus. Jesus has clearly commanded us to reach beyond ourselves and go unto all nations (Matt 28:19). The word "all" means to go "everywhere." God has called us to have a right relationship with the world. After all, "God so loved (not the church but) the world, that he gave his only begotten Son, that whosoever believeth in him should not perish, but have everlasting life" (John 3:16). Even the Greatest Commandment of Love says, "Thou shalt love the Lord thy God with all thy heart, and with all thy soul, and with all thy mind. This is the first and great commandment. And the second is like unto it, Thou shalt love thy neighbour as thyself. On these two commandments hang all the law and the prophets" (Matt 22:37-40).

Often we claim to love God and try to love ourselves, but do not have a right relationship with God because we do not know our neighbor. This can best be illustrated in the scripture narrative of the Good Samaritan in Luke 10:29-35. The question is, "Who is my neighbor?"

> This question, and the answer to this question, is the heart of outreach. It is the question that the legal expert asked Jesus after Jesus told him that to have eternal life, not only must he love God, but he must love his neighbor as himself. When Jesus queried his would-be pupil to see if he understood the story, Jesus asked, 'Which of these...was a neighbor?' The expert answered, 'the one who had mercy...' Jesus then said, 'Go and do likewise.' From Jesus comes every Christian's definition and marching orders, 'Go forth and show mercy.' *A neighbor is anyone who needs help or to be reached.*

> To reach a neighbor, however, one must be a neighbor. Neighbor outreach calls for saved, born-again persons to show mercy by reaching out to a world in need—in physical need and spiritual need. Jesus said, 'The Spirit of the Lord is upon me, because he hath anointed me to preach the gospel to the poor; he hath sent me to heal the brokenhearted, to preach deliverance to the captives, and recovering of sight to the blind, to set at liberty them that are bruised, and to preach the acceptable year of the Lord,' (Luke 4:18,19). Because this is an acceptable year of the Lord, churches ought to do neighborhood outreach.[8]

The key to a right relationship with God is to be involved in missions on foreign soil and at home. Neighborhood outreach is a form of missions. God rewards mission work. A right relationship between the church and the world results in blessings that include church growth.

Suggestions for Implementation

As with each topic of discussion, the ultimate question is, "How do you do it? How do you cherish and prioritize relationships?" Because relationships are activities of the heart, there are no guaranteed methods of implementation. The following helpful suggestions are an attempt to summarize, as well as share some other possible avenues that may result in right relationships for church growth.

Suggestion One: Eliminate voting on people within the church. In most cases, voting on people for offices, positions, or any other reason results in one winner and many losers. There should be no losers in God's family. Voting on people will always damage relationships. Voting on issues can also damage relationships if they are not spiritually discerned. The only vote on a person should come when the church votes to discern the will of God in the calling of a pastor. Afterwards, other methods and procedures should be established to select leadership positions. I fully realize that this may represent a radical change for some churches and denominations, but change is necessary for church growth. If voting on people damages relationships, stifles growth, promotes competition, and establishes a playing field for Satan, it should be eliminated in the church.

Suggestion Two: Tithe the church budget to missions. One of the necessary relationships for church growth is a right relationship between the church and the world. Most churches teach tithing. The church should also be a tither. At least a tenth of the church's budget should be used for missions to insure that the church is in a right relationship with the world. There is a promise of blessings or curses relative to the tithe. "Will a man rob God? Yet ye have robbed me. But ye say, Wherein have we robbed thee? In tithes and offerings. Ye are cursed with a curse: for ye have robbed me, even this whole nation. Bring ye all the tithes into the storehouse, that there may be meat in mine house, and prove me now herewith, saith the LORD of hosts, if I will not open you the windows of heaven, and pour you out a blessing, that there shall not be room enough to receive it" (Mal 3:8-10). This promise is for the body of believers as well as individual saints. Tithing the church budget is one step to help put the church in a right relationship with the world.

Suggestion Three: Teach tithing as a matter of faith rather than a matter of money. Just as tithing the church's budget is essential for the church to have a right relationship with the world, individual tithing puts members in positions to have a right relationship with God. A right relationship with God means trusting God and being dependent upon Him. God challenges us in Malachi 3:10 to try Him and see if He will not open up the windows of heaven. In other words, try Him (tithe), trust Him, depend on Him, see if He will not take care of you and bless you. Members should be encouraged to make commitments to tithe and testimonies about tithing. Tithing puts us in position to have a right relationship with God. Failure to tithe puts us outside the will of God.

Suggestion Four: Preach, teach, and demand obedience to Matt. 18: 15-17. Most believers know that God commands us to love one another. Unfortunately, many are not aware of God's command that we seek to remain in unity one with the other.

Our blueprint for reconciliation is found in Matthew 18:15-17. "Moreover if thy brother shall trespass against thee, go and tell him his fault between thee and him alone: if he shall hear thee, thou hast gained thy brother. But if he will not hear thee, then take with thee one or two more, that in the mouth of two or three witnesses every word may be established. And if he shall neglect to hear them, tell it unto the church: but if he neglect to hear the church, let him be unto thee as an heathen man and a publican." This scripture must be preached and taught. How can God's people obey His command if they do not know His Word? Surprisingly, many church members are not familiar with God's plan for discipline, reconciliation, and forgiveness in the church.

Teaching and preaching this passage are important. However, reconciliation occurs when the truth of this passage is put into practice. The pastor/parent must encourage members to obey this command. The pastor should also remind members that reconciliation is not just between members. The pastor and a member may need to be reconciled, and the pastor must be willing to be reconciled. It is unlikely the congregation will do more than the leader is ready to do. When Matthew 18:15-17 is put into practice, members will be in right relationships with each other and the pastor and in a right relationship with God.

Suggestion Five: Preach and teach prophetically. Prophetic preaching and teaching always call the people back to God. Some teaching simply informs. Often preaching only entertains and inspires. But prophetic teaching and preaching always invite a decision. It is a call for a decision to change and do better. A prophetic ministry of teaching and preaching leads to transformation. Lives are changed. Stewart defines prophetic ministry as "The process of calling the people of God into an awareness of God's saving, liberating and redemptive acts so as to compel the radical participation of individuals and communities in spiritual, social and personal transformation. The result of that transformation will be the realization of human wholeness and potential in the present, as well as in the future."[9] If people are going to experience right relationships, they must be called back into a right relationship with God. Church growth is a result of right relationships with God; therefore, the church must be called to change (transform) and get right with God. This transformation occurs when God's Word is prophetically preached and taught. "For after that in the wisdom of God the world by wisdom knew not God, it pleased God by the foolishness of preaching to save them that believe" (1 Cor. 1:21).

Suggestion Six: Be people-oriented. To be people oriented is to recognize that God so loved the world that He sent His own Son to make known His love for all men. Being "people-oriented" is not the same as being "people-centered." A people-centered view of ministry is not biblical. In a people-oriented approach to church administration, people and their needs are the primary concerns of church administration. People are in no way discriminated against due to sex, race, talents, and socio-economic status. Everything possible is done to protect this principle. Being people-oriented further guards against the church becoming "program-oriented." Programs are for people; people do not exist for programs. Thus, the church should focus on ministries rather than programs, and community rather than committee. In addition, a people-oriented approach underscores the importance of personal relationships as a means of communicating the gospel, thereby developing an alertness to redemptive opportunities in all church settings such as group meetings, recreational activities, etc.

Suggestion Seven: Be administratively organization-conscious. An administration that is well organized promotes and fosters right relationships. This does not mean the church administration must become bureaucratic in character, nor does this undermine or replace our basic theological concept that the church is an *organism* rather than an *organization*. Being organization-conscious means the organizational pattern of the institution helps shape the lives of people. This is contrary to traditional assumptions that individuals shape institutions, and church problems are solved by removing the individual troublemaker, be it the minister, deacon, or disgruntled lay person or group of lay persons. When we are organization-conscious, if a brother or sister is in trouble, we identify the problem in the person, rather than identifying the person as the problem. Effective organizational structure and development is in no way a cure-all for individual problems, and neither is it an attempt to usurp the Holy Spirit nor negate the people-oriented principle. Rather, it is an additional principle of purposeful church administration to aid in the comprehensive movement toward providing experiences that will enable the church to utilize all its resources and personnel in the fulfillment of its mission. For this reason, the church should provide her members with written bylaws setting forth her governance, accompanied by an organizational flow chart. God is not the author of confusion. Peace and harmony within the church encourage growth. Confusion stifles growth. Good organizational administration helps even the playing field for right to always win over wrong.

Suggestion Nine: Create opportunities for the general congregation to show their appreciation and love for the pastor and his family.
A happy first family is directly related to church growth. Most pastors' spouses and children experience some rejection from the church, but they make great sacrifices for the church. The merits of the pastor's appreciation day have been discussed. Other opportunities to show appreciation should also be created. Remember, relationships require effort. We must invest time, energy, and money into relationships. Remembering the pastor's family's birthdays and wedding anniversary and providing adequate compensation for the pastor help foster a right relationship between the members and the pastor.

Suggestion Ten: Assure assimilation through the establishment of small group ministries. This suggestion is discussed in chapters six and seven. Why is this so important that two chapters are required? Because assimilation begins right at the center of our need for relationships, and the utilization of small groups is absolutely necessary to fulfill this need. Be faithful over these two things.

Suggestion Eleven: Emphasize the love and unity aspect of the Holy Communion/Lord's Supper services. The Lord's Supper is a celebration of the death, burial, and resurrection of Christ until His return. Unfortunately, the broken body and spilled blood have become mere symbols that are casually consumed by too many believers in too many churches. If the church and her members are to grow, the meaning of the Lord's Supper must be taught and emphasized.

The Lord's Supper is also a feast of love and unity. Paul writes in 1 Corinthians 10:16-17,

> The cup of blessing which we bless, is it not the communion of the blood of Christ? The bread which we break, is it not the communion of the body of Christ? For we being many are one bread, and one body: for we are all partakers of that one bread.

Notice Paul emphasizes our unity in Christ. The Lord's Supper is a God-ordained and God-instituted practice for building relationships. It is not for physical food. "And if any man hunger, let him eat at home" (1 Cor 11:34a). We are called to examine ourselves before we participate, to determine if our relationships with God and God's people are in order. If they are not we are encouraged to confess our sin and correct our relationships before we partake. "But let a man examine himself, and so let him eat of that bread, and drink of that cup. For he that eateth and drinketh unworthily, eateth and drinketh damnation to himself, not discerning the Lord's body" (1 Cor 11:28-29). This is a serious practice and should not be done routinely or casually.

Churches should periodically include a foot washing service in the Lord's Supper love feast. Jesus washed the feet of His disciples in John 13. Each year on Maundy Thursday Greenforest holds a memorial foot washing service. During this service the pastor washes the feet of the deacons as a visible demonstration of his love for them and his role as chief servant in the church. The deacons and congregation are then encouraged to wash one another's feet in an act of love. Does this sound primitive? Probably. It is biblical.

One of the six essential relationships for church growth is a right relationship between the pastor and the members. The pastor is the undershepherd of the church and the catalyst for correcting and strengthening relationships in the church. While the practice of the pastor's washing the feet of the deacons and other members cannot be evaluated quantitatively, it is related to church growth. One of the barriers to church growth is pride. Every move away from pride and concern for self and toward concern for others and improving relationships within the church family fosters church growth.

<u>Suggestion Twelve: Emphasis on kinship rather than membership</u>.
Membership does not carry the same degree of intimacy as kinship.
Brothers and Sisters in Christ have been born anew in Christ and are,
therefore, related by birth. Churches that emphasize membership are
belittling what God has done through Christ.

Brothers and sisters have certain expectations of themselves
and of each other and strive to protect their relationships. Kinship
relationships can be encouraged in the church by referring to each
other as brother and sister. Many mainline churches have dropped
the practice of naming each other brother and sister because it sounds
primitive, rural, and uneducated. However, this practice is important because it reminds us that we are family, and family is a major
component in relationship building.

Growth-oriented churches make an effort to include singles
in the family. Special ministry attention should be given to singles
because often they are physically separated from their families. Sometimes the separation is emotional. Regardless of the cause of separation, the single members are part of God's family and the church
family. The motto of the singles ministry at Greenforest is "God and
I are a majority." This is a good reminder not only for the single members, but for all members of God's family. Other populations that may
need special ministry attention are the elderly and the physically and
mentally challenged. If the church is to have a right relationship with
God, the entire family must be in a right relationship with each other.

<u>Suggestion Thirteen: Celebrate the arrival of new family members
into the family of God</u>. When a baby is born in a family there is a lot
of excitement. Men pass out cigars to their friends. Grandparents come
quickly to the scene. There are bar mitzvahs for the Jewish boy's arrival into manhood. We have joyous celebrations at graduations and
anniversaries.

What about the arrival of a new brother or sister in God's family? The Bible says the angels are rejoicing (Luke 15:10). We, too, ought
to celebrate. This starts the new relationship on the right foot. When
you begin the right way, the road to maintaining a right relationship
is easier to travel. When someone walks down the aisle and gives his
life to God, the church family should celebrate. When new members
complete the orientation and assimilation process, there should be a
celebration. For example, the right hand of fellowship, which is a
casual practice in some churches, should be emphasized with a
planned event. God wants new additions to His family. That is the

motivation for being faithful over a few things. Why not celebrate the fruit of the labor?

<u>Suggestion Fourteen: Stress family commitments and responsibility.</u> Family implies responsibility. Chores and duties are natural expectations of kinship relationships and strengthen the bonds within the family. In the growth-oriented church, family duties are the commitments that are made by the members. Commitments should not be limited to financial contributions, though these are certainly important. Church family members should be encouraged to make commitments to attend worship services, Sunday School, and Bible studies regularly; to grow in discipleship, prayer, giving, and grace; to evangelize; and to contribute and participate in missions. Our commitments should include the entire work of the church.

If commitments are essential for growth and for strong family relationships, why do so many churches ask so little of the members? Some of the churches have become too sophisticated to ask for commitments from the members. Unfortunately our sophistication has blinded us to the fact that the world views and evaluates the church according to her commitments. Too often, church family members think it is unreasonable to expect them to make commitments to the church yet, they make substantial commitments to secular organizations. The world has seen this low level of commitment and many have concluded that there is no need for the church.

Many of us have simply forgotten that we are a covenant people. God has promised to bless those who keep His covenant. Our right relationship with God depends on this understanding. We must commit to our responsibility to the covenant which puts us in a right relationship with God. Remember, being in a right relationship with God is the main thing of the few things that results in church growth.

<u>Suggestion Fifteen: Become proactive in the area that historically has fostered poor and broken relationships.</u> It has been my observation that there are some areas in the church that historically have been the source of disagreements and poor relationships. Churches can continue to wait until a problem becomes serious and attempt to solve it, or become more proactive and solve or eliminate problems before they occur.

In many churches the choir is a troublesome area. Choir presidents and music directors sometimes fight for control of the choir. At Greenforest Baptist Church we became proactive in this area and simply eliminated the choir offices. This action ended voting for choir officers, reduced conflict in the choir, and prevented disagreements that might occur between the choir officers and the music directors. The result was an environment that is more conducive to developing right relationships.

Another area that can cause broken relationships is voting on nominees during the annual church nominating process. Voting provides an opportunity for politics to enter the church. The church is not an organization; it is an organism. Therefore, politics has no place in the church. While politics may not be eliminated from the church, it can be reduced as much as possible. Instead of voting on members, pray for God to send laborers. Allow those who are willing and are gifted in certain areas to work. There will be certain positions that should only be filled by the pastor. Of course, the congregation should vote to discern God's will in the calling of a pastor.

The issue of the pastor's salary is another area that can polarize the congregation. There will always be a group that is in the pastor's corner, a group that is clearly against the pastor, and the majority of the people who are in the middle and the most vulnerable. The result is polarization, the opposite of unity. The solution is to become proactive and find a method that will eliminate the pastor's salary from becoming a recurring problem. Recurring problems stifle church growth. Harmonious environments promote church growth.

Historically church business meetings have created environments that are not conducive to right relationships and growth. What is the solution? Become proactive and control the environment. Business meetings and church conferences should be replaced with Holy Spirit Discernment Sessions. This is not simply a different name for the same meeting. In business meetings people may try to promote their agendas. In Holy Spirit Discernment Sessions the congregation seeks to discern God's will for the church family. Business is then conducted according to His will, not the congregation's will.

Suggestion Sixteen: Model the Process.   The major premise of this book is the pastor is that the catalyst for church growth. Therefore, all the suggestions of implementation offered in this chapter and the other chapters must be modeled by the pastor first and then the other leadership. We learn best by example. Paul speaks to us about letting our lives be epistles and sermons. A person learns to forgive by seeing forgiveness. Church members learn godly behavior in the midst of evil attacks by watching the pastor stand boldly as fiery darts are being hurled toward him. Members draw strength from other members watching their behavior in the midst of their trials, tribulations and adversities. Model the process for church growth. We let our light shine by modeling the process in all areas of right relationships.

Churches that are concerned about growth must cherish and prioritize relationships. Relationships are the nucleus or heart of church growth. In the next chapter the knowledge-based teaching/ preaching ministry will be presented as the foundation for church growth. From the nucleus (the center) everything else derives its being. The nucleus contains the DNA, the blueprint that will determine what the whole will eventually become. If the heart is right, the whole has the potential to also be right. Contrary, if the heart is not right, the whole will be wrong. Right does not grow from wrong.

Right Relationships as the Essential Thing of the Few Things. Since the opposite of relationship is self-sufficiency, which is the nucleus of wrong and evil, relationship is not only one of the few things, it is the essential thing. Peter had broken his relationship with Jesus by denying him three times. In the process of restoring that relationship Jesus asked him, not one time, but three times, "Peter do you love Me.?" Jesus goes on the say, "If you really love me, feed my sheep." The question to us is the same today. Christ is asking pastors, churches, and church leaders, "Do you love me?" If so, get right with Me and help Me grow My church. Cherish and prioritize relationships. A right relationship with God is the essential thing of a few faithful things that will cause churches to grow.

In Summary

Building relationships should be the number one goal of the church. Relationships can be defined in terms of a bonding connection as in kinship or family. Relationships are so important that they must be cherished and nurtured. In this chapter, five stages of relationship development were analyzed. The key components that define godly relationships—people, love, bonding, and family were thoroughly examined. Six kinds of relationships were explained, and the relevance of the Ten Commandments to relationships was noted. Sixteen suggestions for implementation were set forth with a rationale and explanation. A right relationship with God was proposed as the essential thing of a few things that will cause the church to grow.

Chapter 2

Establishing a Knowledge-Based Teaching/Preaching Foundation

Four Reasons for a Knowledge-Based Teaching/Preaching Foundation

God-ordained church growth has as its foundation the knowledge-based ministries of teaching and preaching. There are four reasons why growing churches must be faithful to these ministries. (1) God's will is that we teach.(2) A knowledge-based foundation keeps the focus on Christ and not on the leader. (3) It is the preaching of the gospel that is the power unto salvation. (4) A knowledge-based foundation provides stability during times of adversity that allows the church to continue to grow.

Reason One - God's Will

Jesus, as teacher, was often referred to as rabbi in the New Testament. Rabbi translates to teacher. Speaking of Nicodemus, John's gospel records: "The same came to Jesus by night, and said unto him, Rabbi, we know that thou art a teacher come from God" (John 3:2). The central thread that weaves throughout Jesus' earthly ministry is teaching.

"And Jesus went about all Galilee, *teaching* in their synagogues, and preaching the gospel of the kingdom, and healing all manner of sickness and all manner of disease among the people" (Matt 4:23).

Likewise when He gave His "Sermon on the Mount" His posture was that of teacher: "And he opened his mouth, and *taught* them, saying," (Matt 5:2).

When he finished the lesson on building on a solid (rock) foundation, the scripture records: "For he *taught* them as one having authority, and not as the scribes" (Matt 7:29).

From Mark's gospel, before He fed five thousand we find these words: "And Jesus, when he came out, saw much people, and was moved with compassion toward them, because they were as sheep not having a shepherd: and he began to *teach* them many things" (Mark 6:34).

After Jesus was tempted by Satan in the wilderness for 40 days and before His first recorded act of ministry He, "returned in the power of the Spirit into Galilee: and there went out a fame of him through all the region round about. And he *taught* in their synagogues, being glorified of all" (Luke 4:14-15).

In John's gospel we find Jesus teaching in the temple: "Now about the midst of the feast Jesus went up into the temple, and *taught*" (John 7:14).

And on the Mount of Olives prior to His lesson on the universality of sin relative to the forgiveness of the adulterous woman, we find Jesus still in the mode of teacher: "And early in the morning he came again into the temple, and all the people came unto him; and he sat down, and *taught* them" (John 8:2).

In addition to Jesus' example, the Bible provides four "Great" events and admonitions that indicate that it is God's will for us to teach.
1.   The Great Commission
2.   The Great Confession
3.   The Greatest Commandment
4.   The Great Growth Commission

The Great Commission (Matt. 28:19-20)

"Go ye therefore, and teach all nations, baptizing them in the name of the Father, and of the Son, and of the Holy Ghost: Teaching them to observe all things whatsoever I have commanded you: and, lo, I am with you alway, even unto the end of the world. Amen."

The Great Commission is not a divine suggestion. This is a commandment. It is correctly translated not "go" but "as you are going," teach. As you are going make disciples. As you are going, make obedient learners and followers. This was Christ's last commandment before He ascended into heaven to sit at the right hand of God the Father. It is Christ's will that we teach.

The Great Confession

Jesus asked the disciples the most important question in the world, "Whom do men say that I the Son of man am?" (Matt. 16:13). More specifically He further asked, "But whom say ye that I am?" (Matt 16:15). The Great Confession followed, "And Simon Peter answered and said, Thou art the Christ, the Son of the living God" (Matt. 16:16). Jesus' response was that the Holy Spirit through the Father taught Him the answer, because the answer could not have come from flesh and blood: "And Jesus answered and said unto him, Blessed art thou, Simon Barjona: for flesh and blood hath not revealed it unto thee, but my Father which is in heaven"(Matt. 16:17).

One of the functions of the Holy Spirit today is to teach: "But the Comforter, which is the Holy Ghost, whom the Father will send in my name, he shall teach you all things, and bring all things to your remembrance, whatsoever I have said unto you" (John 14:26). God the Father teaches: "And thou shalt speak unto him, and put words in his mouth: and I will be with thy mouth, and with his mouth, and will teach you what ye shall do" (Exo. 4:15). God the Father, God the Son, and God the Holy Ghost teach. It is clearly God's will that we teach.

The Greatest Commandment

God the Father said, "...Thou shall teach them diligently" (Deut. 6:7). Teach them what? To "... love the LORD thy God with all thine heart, and with all thy soul, and with all thy might" (Deut 6:5). Later, in the New Testament, the same God now robed in flesh as God the Son gave the same commandment from the posture of teacher. A lawyer trying to tempt or confuse Jesus asked Him a question. Addressing Him as "Master" (that may be interpreted "Teacher"), he asked, "Master, which is the great commandment in the law? Jesus said unto him, "Thou shalt love the Lord thy God with all thy heart, and with all thy soul, and with all thy mind. This is the first and great commandment. And the second is like unto it, Thou shalt love thy neighbour as thyself. On these two commandments hang all the law and the prophets" (Matt 22:36-40). Two points are noteworthy. First, because the Savior was Master or Teacher he could not be tempted, tricked, or confused by a lawyer or the law. Second, Jesus gave us the greatest commandment from the posture of teaching. God wants us to teach!

The Great Growth Commission

The textural narrative for the Great Growth Commission is found in Luke 5:1-11. The narrative concludes with Jesus' invitation for the fishermen to become catchers of men and follow Him. Observe the setting and the posture of Jesus as He led them to (1) stop washing their nets, (2) get in the boat, (3) launch out into deep water, and (4) let down their nets. Jesus entered the boat, "And he sat down, and taught the people out of the ship" (Luke 5:3c). He taught them. Jesus was a teacher, and He wants us to teach.

Great is our God. Great is His word. Great is His purpose. Great is our responsibility. Great is His will. His will is for us to teach. How do we best carry out this will? We must be faithful to establish a knowledge-based teaching/preaching foundation to assure His teaching "will" will be done.

Reason Two - Jesus Focused

The second reason why God-ordained growth requires a knowledge-based teaching/preaching foundation is to keep the focus on Jesus. Christ is the Cornerstone and Foundation. He is also the Head. The Head must always wag the tail, rather than the reverse. All principles of growth must be Christ-centered. The church's mission statement should clearly articulate that Christ is the head of the church. Everything we do must be determined by the Head. When the church's agenda becomes the same as Jesus' agenda, the church will grow.

In the building of anything the foundation is of utmost importance. A house or garage or church will eventually fall unless the foundation is solid. One of the basic assumptions of this book is that the pastor is the catalyst for church growth. The pastor is the orchestra conductor. He ignites, motivates, and orchestrates the building of God's kingdom at the level of the local church. The danger of this truism is apparent when pastors depart. Case studies of once growing churches that are now dead or declining can easily be cited. Why did these churches stop growing? In many instances the decline was the result of the pastor's departure. Although the pastor is the number one agent of church growth, he should never be the foundation. No matter how skilled, charismatic, or gifted, the pastor should never become the church's foundation. The church must assure herself that Jesus, not the pastor or any other component of the church, is indeed the main attraction. The songwriter put it best by penning:

> The Church's One Foundation is Jesus Christ her Lord;
> She is His new creation by water and the Word
> From heav'n He came and sought her to be His holy bride;
> With His own blood He bought her, and for her life He died.[10]

Churches often attempt to build on the gifts and talents in the church such as the oratorical gift of the pastor, musical gifts of the choir, business expertise of the trustees, spiritual gift of tongues, or charismatic gifts of the leaders. This growth at best will be temporary. Only what you do for Christ will last. God promises throughout His word that the only thing that will stand the test of time is His *word*.

Psalm 119:89	For ever, O LORD, thy *word* is settled in heaven.
Isaiah 40:8	The grass withereth, the flower fadeth: but the *word* of our God shall stand for ever.
Mark 13:31	Heaven and earth shall pass away: but my *words* shall not pass away.
1 Peter 1:25	But the *word* of the Lord endureth for ever. And this is the word which by the gospel is preached unto you.

The Word is eternal. The Word was pre-existent. The Word was with God in the beginning and will be with God for all time. In the fullness of time, The Word became flesh. Jesus is The Word and Jesus is God incarnate; "In the beginning was the Word, and the Word was with God, and the Word was God. And the Word was made flesh, and dwelt among us, (and we beheld his glory, the glory as of the only begotten of the Father), full of grace and truth" (John 1:1,14). Therefore the church must be based on The Word. Growing churches that expect to stand the test of time, as well as grow according to the will of God, must establish a knowledge (Word)-based foundation.

The apostle tells the church in Corinth that "For other foundation can no man lay than that is laid, which is Jesus Christ" (1 Cor
3:11). Paul goes on to say we should be careful how we build our
ministries. Some will build with gold or precious stone that will stand
the test of fire, while others will build with hay, wood, stubble, and
straw that will not stand the test. The major point is that regardless of
how you build or what material you use, you must have Christ as the
foundation. Over and over again, the New Testament tells us of the
necessity of having Christ as the foundation of our existence.

> "Therefore thus saith the Lord GOD, Behold, I lay in Zion
> for a foundation a stone, a tried stone, a precious corner
> stone, a sure foundation: he that believeth shall not make
> haste" (Isa 28:16).

> "Laying up in store for themselves a good foundation
> against the time to come, that they may lay hold on eternal
> life" (1 Tim 6:19).

> "Nevertheless the foundation of God standeth sure, hav-
> ing this seal, The Lord knoweth them that are his" (2 Tim
> 2:19a).

The narrative in Matt. 7:24-25 and the parallel version in Luke
6:48 make it very clear that we must build our ministry on a foundation of solid rock.

> "Therefore whosoever heareth these sayings of mine, and
> doeth them, I will liken him unto a wise man, which built
> his house upon a rock: And the rain descended, and the
> floods came, and the winds blew, and beat upon that house;
> and it fell not: for it was founded upon a rock" (Matt 7:24,25).

Notice three things in Matthew 7:24-25. First, the rain, the rising
water, and the wind came against both the house on sand and the
house on the rock. The only difference is the house built on the rock
stood. Trials and tribulations are inevitable. Whether we stand or fall
depends on the foundation. Second, if it is inevitable that storms are
a part of church growth, why wait until the storm comes before you
strengthen the foundation? Begin building your ministry on a knowledge-based foundation immediately. Third, the strengthening pro-

cess is a continuous process. Unlike a physical building where you may be able to dig the foundation and pour the concrete one time, building spiritual temples is an ongoing process. Therefore, the church's knowledge-based teaching/preaching foundation should represent an ongoing crusade of teaching and learning opportunities.

The lesson is clear. Build only on The Word. Build only on Christ. Build on the Rock. Stand on the Solid Rock. Join the songwriter in his proclamation "On Christ the Solid Rock I stand, all other ground is sinking sand."[11] Establish a knowledge-based teaching/preaching foundation.

Reason Three - The Preaching of the Gospel as the Power Unto Salvation

The third reason why churches must be faithful in establishing a knowledge-based teaching/ preaching foundation is that the preaching of the gospel is the power unto salvation. The Bible clearly says "...it pleased God by the foolishness of preaching to save them that believe" (1 Cor. 1:21b). In the Book of Romans, God also declares, "For whosoever shall call upon the name of the Lord shall be saved. How then shall they call on him in whom they have not believed? And how shall they believe in him of whom they have not heard? And how shall they hear without a preacher"(Rom. 10: 13-14)?

It is difficult to separate teaching from preaching. For the purposes of this book preaching is the activity that takes place during regular worship services at the point and time when the pastor stands to proclaim (preach) God's word. God holds the pastor responsible for being faithful in the utilization of this time. "Take heed therefore unto yourselves, and to all the flock, over the which the Holy Ghost hath made you overseers, to feed the church of God, which he hath purchased with his own blood" (Acts 20:28).

The *what* of preaching is more important than the *how* of preaching. *How* is related to style. It is true that many talented preachers have been able to grow churches because of their preaching ability. It is also true that these churches oftentimes decline when the pastor leaves the church. The *what* of preaching deals with the content. The content should be aimed at transformation. Purposeful preaching asks for commitments to become more like Christ.

More messages and fewer sermons should be preached. Sermons are about God and the history of redemption. Sermons seldom call for a decision or a commitment. But messages are about what God has to say to us today based on who He is and what He has done. Messages start with Jesus, make a beeline to the cross with a contemporary word of substance from God along the way, and end with the power and love of God as dessert. Messages always ask for a decision from nonbelievers and members. Nonbelievers should be encouraged to accept Christ. All members should be asked to make the decision to grow in their faith.

Pastors who are sincere about growing churches should also spend less time studying and imitating the preaching style of pastors of growing churches and more time studying their leadership styles. Leadership style is a more important factor in church growth than preaching style.

Reason Four - Stability

Trials and tribulations are a natural part of growth. In fact we often refer to them as growing pains. A growing church will have growing pains. When the winds blow, the storms come, and growing pains surface, the church that is not built on a strong foundation will crumble and fall. Establishing a knowledge-based teaching/preaching foundation is necessary for churches to grow at their full potential, as well as maintain their growth over time.

While knowledge alone cannot produce a new birth or transformation, it is a necessary part of the process. How can a church move forward and members grow if ignorance is in the driver's seat? Paul tells us to "be not conformed to this world: but be ye transformed by the renewing of your mind" (Rom 12:2). Knowledge of God is essential for the renewal of our minds.

Hosea warns us in the Old Testament proclamation, "My people are destroyed for lack of knowledge: because thou hast rejected knowledge, I will also reject thee, that thou shalt be no priest to me: seeing thou hast forgotten the law of thy God, I will also forget thy children" (Hosea 4:6). There are three important points about the lack of knowledge in this passage.

First, it is destructive: *"My people are destroyed for lack of knowledge."* The question may be asked, "How can a lack of anything destroy?" How can nothing hurt anything? Without the sun all life is destroyed. Without the Son of God all would die and go to hell. Without knowledge of God we have no standard for living, therefore we are destroyed. We must have knowledge of the law before we can be obedient to the law; "Behold, to obey is better than sacrifice," (1 Sam

15:22). The soul without knowledge of God is like a plant without water and an animal without air.

Second, lack of knowledge is willful: *"because thou hast rejected knowledge."* There is no excuse for ignorance of the knowledge of God. God has not hidden His knowledge from us. God reveals Himself to us in nurture and in nature. His word even declares the availability of His knowledge. "For the invisible things of him from the creation of the world are clearly seen, being understood by the things that are made, even his eternal power and Godhead; so that they are without excuse:" (Rom 1:20).

Third, lack of knowledge of God is offensive to God: *"I will also reject thee."* In other words, God is displeased when we reject His knowledge. It is impossible to please Him without faith and He is not pleased when we are ignorant of His knowledge. Therefore, one cannot be faithful over a few things without knowledge of God: *"that thou shalt be no priest to me."*

Hosea provides a special word of caution to pastors and other ordained (set apart) servants. There is at least one interpretation of Hosea 4:6 that places the burden of accountability and responsibility on the priests (ordained servants). With no attempt to theologize, this should at least draw attention to the responsibility of the pastor and church to teach. Oftentimes I hear pastors complain that their congregations are ignorant. Whose fault is it? Who is to blame? The people of God allow the pastor to be their center of attention at least once a week during the prime time hour of 11 o'clock on Sunday morning. All attention is focused on the pastor and the pulpit for at least one hour. My point is that pastors should use the pulpit as a teaching station. In fact the pulpit should be the number one teaching station in the church, not the Sunday School, the discipleship training class, nor the pastor's Bible study class. God holds the pastor accountable. This is one of the few things the pastor must do to be faithful over the few things necessary for church growth—that is, teach from the pulpit during prime time.

Establishing a Knowledge-Based Teaching/Preaching Foundation—How?

How do you establish a knowledge-based teaching foundation?

1. Make the teaching ministry one of the major identification labels of the church.

2.   Make Christian education the undergirding ministry for all the other ministries in the church.
3.   Create an ongoing teaching crusade in the church.
4.   Remember the power of the pulpit.

The Teaching Ministry as an Identification Label. The teaching ministry should be one of the major identification labels of the church. A label of identification is that for which the church is known. A good identification label is a strong teaching ministry. People are hungry for the Word. Cults are benefiting from this hunger for knowledge and our negligence. In fact, many popular cults report that the majority of their new recruits are from mainline churches that are not satisfying people's hunger for the Word. Let God's true church be known as a teaching church.

Christian Education as an Undergirding Ministry. The church becomes a teaching church when the ministry of Christian education undergirds all the other ministries of the church. While in seminary, I was blessed to take a course in Christian education, in which the instructor repeated the definition of Christian education daily. He literally said at least ten times each day during the semester, "Christian education is that ministry of the church that undergirds all the other ministries of the church."[12] The repetition became boring and taken by many of the students as a laughing matter. However, it became the compass for my pastorate. Why is Christian education so important? An undergirding Christian education ministry provides a sure foundation. Disagreement in a growing church is expected. When the winds blow and the church storms arise, the church may bend but not break if the foundation is strong. If Christian education has undergirded all the other ministries of the church, the winds will not blow as intensely, and the water will not rise enough to be harmful. For example, if the majority of the choir members are involved in the Christian education ministry, a conflict in the choir is more likely to be resolved or managed than if the majority of the choir members only attend the worship service.

  Christian education also undergirds the stewardship of the church. People become good stewards when they are taught to be good stewards by the Word of God. Furthermore, Christian education undergirds the facilities and maintenance ministry of the church. People will learn to take care of the church when they are taught to take care of the church. The Christian education ministry should even undergird the worship ministry. People will only praise and celebrate the goodness of God in public worship if they are taught to do so. Christian education is that ministry of the church that undergirds all the other ministries of the church.

Create an Ongoing Teaching Crusade. The third suggestion offered concerning the implementation of a knowledge-based teaching/preaching foundation is to create an ongoing teaching crusade in the church. In other words, teaching is taking place at every level, every day, and all the time.
     To illustrate and further explain the nature and scope of the teaching crusade, the Greenforest Baptist Church model is offered.

> **The Mission of Greenforest Baptist Church** is to be Christ-centered and Bible-based; make disciples for Christ; minister to the hurts and hopes of the community; and provide opportunities for authentic expressive worship.

> **The Mission of the Christian Education Ministry** is to undergird all the other ministries of the Church by teaching the people of God to obey the commands of God.

This ongoing teaching focus is represented in the following Christian Education Organization Chart. (The components have been given an alphabetical listing for clarification and discussion purposes).

CHRISTIAN EDUCATION ORGANIZATION CHART

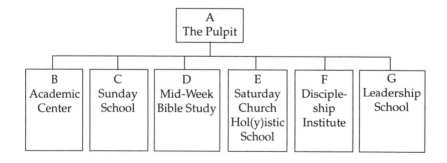

A. The Pulpit. As previously discussed, the pulpit is foremost a teaching station, for that is where teaching begins. Each message has an identifiable spiritual truth to be learned.

B. The Christian Academic Center. The Greenforest Christian Academic Center is committed to producing graduates who demonstrate superior academic achievement and the desire to serve God and mankind. Presently, nearly 600 students are enrolled in preschool through 12th grade. The Academic Center's mission statement is as follows:

> **The Mission Statement of the Greenforest Christian Academic Center** is to produce Christian graduates who demonstrate superior academic achievement as measured by results of teacher-made tests, standardized assessments, and regional and national competitions; also, to instill in our children the knowledge of who they are and whose they are, demonstrated by their desire to serve God and mankind.

The Abeka curriculum is utilized and supplemented with curricula that will help our students accelerate in math and the other sciences, as well as ensure that they will be prepared to continue their education in whichever institution of higher learning they wish to attend. The Academic Center provides an alternative to public schools. Classes meet daily at regular school hours. In most cases, classroom facilities are shared with Sunday School classes, Wednesday Bible study classes, discipleship training and Saturday church school classes.

C. Sunday School. The purpose of the Sunday School is to provide an opportunity for the laity to fulfill the functional purposes of the church, namely, reaching, teaching, fellowshiping, and nurturing. Notice, the Sunday School should be a ministry of the laity; therefore, the pastor must be careful to remain in the role of facilitator or coach and not dictator. To the extent feasible, the Sunday School should be operated by the lay ministry. Dr. Gene Mims, Vice President of the Baptist Sunday School Board, in his book entitled *Kingdom Principles for Church Growth* lists the following five essential church functions for church growth: (1) Evangelism, (2) Discipleship, (3) Ministry, (4) Fellowship, and (5) Worship.[13] The growth-oriented Sunday School ministry fulfills four of the five functions.

The growth-oriented Sunday School (G.O.S.S.) is purposefully organized to grow. Growth principles are set forth and implemented to promote growth. The impact of the Sunday School on church growth can best be illustrated in a typical G.O.S.S. organization chart and the nine growth principles that follow.

SUNDAY SCHOOL ORGANIZATION CHART

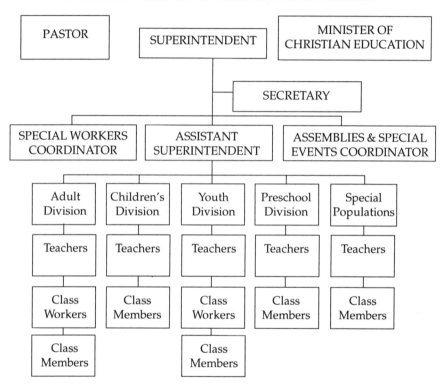

NINE PRINCIPLES OF SUNDAY SCHOOL GROWTH

1. Make a commitment to growth.
2. Identify and enroll prospects.
3. Start new classes and departments.
4. Enlist workers.
5. Train workers.
6. Provide space and equipment.
7. Conduct weekly workers meeting.
8. Conduct weekly visitations.
9. Teach the Bible to win the lost and develop the saved. [14]

If the Sunday School is organized in the above manner and the Sunday School growth principles are implemented, the Sunday School will grow. If the Sunday School grows, the church grows. If quality teaching supported by discipleship training is assured, the Sunday School will grow qualitatively and quantitatively and the church will experience spiritual and numerical growth.

D. Mid-Week Bible Study. The purpose of the mid-week Bible study is to provide a specific time and call to obtain biblical knowledge through a variety of Bible study methods. There are many effective ways to study the Bible. Classes are designed in content and method to reach a diverse population according to age, interest, and learning and teaching preferences. There is something offered for everyone, members and visitors, on Wednesday evening .Some of the classes offered are General Bible Study, Devotional Bible Study, Bible Exposition, Basic Bible Interpretation, and the Bible Verse by Verse, as well as children's and youth classes by age groupings. Some teachers teach more effectively through the lecture style, while other teachers are more effective as guided discovery teachers or facilitators. The idea is to match the learner's most effective way of learning with a teacher's strongest teaching style.

The purpose of mid-week Bible study is to provide a call to the saints to gather for the purpose of gathering biblical knowledge. Granted, one can and should study the Bible at home and alone, but growing churches always call for commitment and accountability. The church gathers on Wednesday night. The saints come together for Bible study, not worship. The call for Bible study is for only one hour, 7:30 to 8:30. From 6:30 to 7:30 other church activities can take place such as Sunday School workers meeting or deacon cluster meeting. From 8:30 to 9:30 occasionally there are special worship services.

The 7:30 to 8:30 hour is for Bible study. Traditional prayer meeting behaviors are discouraged during the Bible study time. The emphasis is on teaching and learning. This is not mid-week prayer meeting, this is mid-week Bible study. No more than ten minutes should be spent on prayer requests, prayer and devotion. At least 50 of the 60 minutes allotted should be spent in quality Bible study. Mid-week Bible study, unlike Sunday School, is singularly focused. Teaching is the only objective of mid-week Bible study, not fellowship, nurturing, evangelism, or worship. The mid-week Bible study is a major artery in the teaching ministry.

E. The Saturday Church Hol(y)istic School. The purpose of the Saturday Church Hol(y)istic School is to provide an opportunity for the church and her members to give back and share their gifts, talents and blessings from God by ministering holistically to the needs, hopes and hurts of the membership and the community. There are no paid teachers in the Saturday Hol(y)istic School. The idea is to bless others as God has blessed us by ministering to others. The word hol(y)istic grew out of the heartfelt desire not to be confused with the New Age movement and similar religious groups that articulate considerable rhetoric concerning holistic ministering. This is not a self-centered ministry. This a Christ-centered ministry, thus the name hol(y)istic rather than holistic. Courses are offered, however, that may not be specifically Bible-oriented, such as computer basics, preparation for the Scholastic Aptitude Test, music note reading, sign language, arts and crafts, aerobics, and math and English tutoring. The basic criterion is that a class must be instructional and in keeping with the mission of the church to minister to the needs, hopes and hurts of the community.

Saturday Church Hol(y)istic School is also a major artery in the ongoing teaching crusade. The designated time slot at Greenforest Baptist Church for Saturday Hol(y)istic School is 12 noon to 2 p.m. No other activities such as choir rehearsals, ministry meetings committee meetings, athletic competitions, etc., are permitted to be held during this time which has been designated for instructional activity only.

F. Discipleship Institute.

The Mission Statement of the Discipleship Institute is to provide progressive, graded, need-specific discipleship instruction in large or small class settings; to encourage and hold each other accountable in small groups; and to disciple others individually.

Our definition of a disciple is one who is a disciplined learner and follower of Christ who teaches another to become a disciplined learner and follower of Christ. One must make a disciple in order to be a disciple. One of the greatest convicting moments I have experienced in my pastorate was when I understood that I had been spending too much time making converts and not enough time making disciples. As mentioned earlier, the biblical mandate from The Great Commission is to make disciples, not converts or church members.

The discipleship training ministry at Greenforest Baptist Church is the capstone of the teaching crusade. Discipleship groups, called "D" groups, take place anywhere and at any time other than the designated time for Sunday School. The discipleship classes offered such as MasterLife I and II, a course sequence produced by the Sunday School Board of the Southern Baptist Convention, have been carefully selected from a variety of discipleship courses to fulfill the stated mission of the ministry.

The discipleship curriculum first helps members determine their level of spiritual maturity. Next members are guided and challenged to progress at their own rate of speed, desire, and determination through various maturation levels of discipleship.

G. Leadership School. The Leadership School was established to (1) identify potential leaders in the congregation, (2) help these individuals develop leadership skills and lead their ministry groups through various training modules, and (3) provide opportunities for all church leaders to examine God's work for the church and the importance of becoming servant leaders. Leadership classes are held on fourth Sunday evenings.

Remember the Power of the Pulpit.   Preaching is the most powerful tool God has ordained. The pulpit becomes powerful when God's anointed messenger or vessel delivers God's anointed word. The vessel and the message must be prepared for the pulpit.

Depending on the experience and skills of the pastor, the time required to prepare a 20 to 40 minute sermon can vary from 20 to 40 hours. Sundays come quickly for the busy pastor. Do not cheapen God's word by doing so many things other than sermon preparation that adequate time is not allowed for the preparation of God's preached word. In addition, be careful not to crowd the worship time period with activities that reduce the time allowed for preaching.

Preaching requires physical energy, thus exercise, rest, and proper nutrition are very important. Take care of your body.

In addition to the physical requirements of preaching, the pastor must be prepared spiritually. Spend time with God before you enter your library and before you enter the pulpit. Scholarly research is important, but the anointing makes the difference. We must remember that preaching is the power of God through a human vessel. The vessel must be cleansed and made ready to deliver the message. Remember the power of the pulpit. Be prepared to be used by God to teach His people. Be faithful over this one of few things.

In Summary

Growing churches must be faithful to building on a solid foundation. First, it is God's will that we teach. Second, a knowledge-based teaching/preaching foundation keeps the focus on Christ and not on the pastor. Third, the preaching of the gospel is the power unto salvation. Finally, a knowledge-based teaching/preaching foundation provides stability that allows the church to continue to grow in time of adversity. In this chapter, all of the above reasons were examined and discussed. Four suggestions for the implementation of a knowledge-based teaching/preaching foundation were examined, explored and discussed.

Chapter 3

Initiate Change

If I were asked to identify the primary reason churches do not grow or will not grow, I would say it is because of their inability to change. All church growth principles, methods, procedures and strategies are worthless if change cannot be initiated. When I travel across this country speaking and participating in church growth conferences, the pastors and lay persons I meet seem to be sincere in their desire for the church to grow. They are excited about new methods and strategies. They want to hurry back to their local church to begin implementation. Yet, when they return, they are met with resistance. Let us be honest; humans do not like to change. In fact, we resist change. Most of us like to wear the same clothes, eat the same food, and what is more convincing, sit in the same seat, even in church. Psychologists theorize that our need for a security blanket and our space causes us to resist change.

Reasons People Resist Change

According to Lovett H. Weems, Jr., the ten most common reasons people resist change are these: (1) It makes people feel out of control. People tighten up when they feel powerless. (2) There is too much uncertainty. What will it mean for them? Is it safe? (3) They have never heard it before. People do not respond well when asked for reaction on the spot. The ground must first be prepared. (4) It disrupts routine. The known and certain are appealing; (5) It makes people lose face. It seems as if what they did in the past was wrong. (6) It makes people feel uncertain about their competence. (7) There is a ripple effect on other people and their efforts. It disrupts other things. (8) Things that are new require more work. People feel they have no reason to put in the extra effort. (9) There is a chip on the shoulder from the past. People are angry because of something else. (10) Sometimes the threat is real. The great idea will hurt someone else. There are few totally positive ideas.[15]

I have experienced most of these responses to change. The most frequent reactions have been fear of the unknown, never heard of it being done that way, more work required, and saving face for what was previously done. The discussion that follows addresses the most common experiences.

First, people do not like to change because they are afraid of change. This is understandable. The unknown has always caused fear. It has been said that knowledge replaces fear. But I am reminded of the scripture that tells us that, "perfect love casts out fear." How so? Because to love God is to trust God. When people learn to love God and learn to love as God loves, change becomes more acceptable. A key component in this process is realizing that people must learn to love God. Paul states in Philippians 4:11, "I have learned...." People *learn* to love God. In Deuteronomy 6:5-7a we read: "And thou shalt love the Lord thy God with all thine heart, and with all thy soul, and with all thy might. And these words, which I command thee this day, shall be in thine heart: And thou shalt teach them diligently...." Teach them what? Teach them to love God. We are called by The Great Commission to observe His commandments and the greatest of these commandments is to love God. People resist change because of fear. People change because of their love for God. Perfect love casts out fear. To perfectly love God is to trust God. To trust God is to permit God to guide in various directions as He sees fit. Thus, change can be initiated.

Second, people resist change because they have never done it that way or heard of it done that way before. Again, this is a result of an attempt to control God and maintain an environment of self-control. How often do we try to remain in control while giving lip service to the fact that God cannot be put in a matchbox. Our arms have always been too short to box with God. God cannot be confined. He cannot be locked up today any more than He could nearly two thousand years ago when He broke out of a new rock-hewn tomb.

I saw a quote once that read, "Dumb defined: Doing the same thing over and over again and expecting different results." A good reason for change, even if you have never done it that way before, is the fact that what you currently are doing is failing. To continue to do it the same way over and over again, expecting it to work when it has not in the past, fits the definition of dumb.

Third, the thought of more work being required is yet another reason why people resist change. Two things need to happen for this barrier to be overcome. Either the people have to change or leadership needs to change the people. In other words, if the motivation is not there and cannot be initiated, then a new set of people must become the catalyst for the momentum and implementation of change. One of the realities of church growth is that new members are the lifeblood of change. This is a sensitive area, for truly God has called the pastor and church leaders to love and minister to all members equally. Yet pastors of growing churches need to prioritize their time to spend more time with new members. The pastor of a growing church would benefit more from teaching the new member orientation class than an established Sunday School pastor's class.

Sometimes those who are using the existing method, strategy, or process will resist change because they equate system change and system failure. If the system failed, are they failures as well? Of course not. Yet, the people involved may think they will be viewed as failures. Their responses may be embarrassment, or they may be insulted by the change. Principles fail. This is not an indicator that people have failed. However, it is often perceived that way, and perceptions are real in the mind of the beholder. During periods of change, fine well-meaning members may get hurt. This is not good and can be minimized. Their resistance can be overcome through love, gentleness, and diplomacy of the leadership.

To successfully initiate change, the leader should be prepared to answer four questions concerning the proposed changes. They are (1) Why change? (2) What needs changing? (3) What needs changing most? (4) How do we best implement change?

The Need to Change

Why change? Should we change for the sake of changing. No! However, a case could be made for change based on our changing society. Because society is changing, some changes must occur in the church. Why change when most people in church are satisfied? Why change when most people in church are happy and comfortable with the status quo? Herein lies one of the greatest sins of the church today--the sin of apathy and indifference. The prophet Amos warned the northern tribes of Israel (now often referred to as the ten lost tribes of Israel), "Woe to them that are at ease in Zion" (Amos 6:1).

We live in a secular world where ease has become a merit. The world values ease: the Life of Riley, the La-Z-Boy chair, easy job, easy money, easy cooking, easy living, and yes, even easy church. Churches with no call for commitments are popular. Churches that have no expectation for righteous living are appealing, and churches that do not challenge members to change to meet the needs of a changing society are desirable. Woe unto us that are too comfortable in our churches. God wants us holy before we are happy; and if we are holy we will be happy. Everlasting joy is found in holiness. Change is inevitable if we are to become holy in Christ, and change is inevitable if we are to be in His will. The changes I have and continue to institute in my pastorate (and there are many) are all directed from my discernment of God's will. I sincerely believe that the number one reason why I have been blessed to pastor a church God is growing is due to my obedience to God's will and my faith that God will take care of me if I am courageous enough to implement change.

Lyle E. Schaller discusses several reasons for change in his monthly *Parish Paper.*

1. Change usually must be one component of a larger strategy by any long-established congregation that seeks to reach newer generations of people.
2. Change usually is a part of a larger strategy to challenge people with a new vision of what tomorrow could be.
3. Change is an essential component of any strategy to focus a congregation's agenda on ministry and outreach.
4. A reason for change is in response to discontentment.
5. A reason to change is when the old system does not work.
6. A reason for change is to keep up with the competition.

Reasons four, five and six are true, pragmatic, and obvious. However, reasons one through three seem to be less obvious and pragmatic, and more theological and spiritual; thus, they deserve additional discussion.

First, change is necessary to reach newer generations of people for Christ. The issue is more than a pragmatic issue. It is a spiritual issue. The real issue, then, for many of the older generations is do they love Jesus and His Word enough that they are willing to change for Him? Salvation is not a method. Christ did not specify methods and procedures for salvation. I am reminded of the scripture narrative wherein Jesus healed the demonic man named Legend. Jesus cast out his demons into the swine and the swine ran into the river. The man was a new creature now "clothed in his right mind" (Mark 5:15, Luke 8:35). However, when the town folk saw him clothed in his right mind, they were more concerned about the pigs than they were joyful about the changed man. One can easily surmise that they must have loved material things (ham, pork chops, bacon, etc.) more than they loved salvation and Jesus.

Do we refuse to change because of love of self more than love of Jesus? Are we willing to change for God's sake to save newer generations? Refusal to do so because we like the way things are is self-centered and sinful. Remember, God calls us to holiness before happiness. Newer generations include baby boomers and baby busters. The majority of church members that control mainline churches are neither baby boomers or busters. They are depression and borderline depression babies. There is as serious a generation gap between a depression baby and baby busters. But the call for and the need for salvation is the same today as yesterday. Likewise, God's Word (Jesus Christ) is "the same yesterday, and today, and forever" (Heb 13:8). The message is the same but the methods can be and must be changed from generation to generation to meet the generational changes.

The second reason for change is theological. The foundation of Christianity is the supernatural changing power of God. "Behold, I was shapen in iniquity; and in sin did my mother conceive me" (Psalm 51:5). Yet, by the demonstrated love of God through Christ Jesus and the power of the Holy Ghost, we have become new creatures in Him. Biblically, we are admonished, "be not conformed to this world: but be ye transformed by the renewing of your mind, that ye may prove what is that good, and acceptable, and perfect, will of God (Rom. 12:2). Change was necessary for Christians to become who we are. But the process of change does not end at the point of becoming a Christian because we are commanded to make disciples. Being a disciple of Christ is an ever growing transformation process--becoming more and more like Him. Also, Christianity anticipates the promise of the mystery of change associated with eternal life. "Behold, I shew you a mystery; We shall not all sleep, but we shall all be changed, In a moment, in the twinkling of an eye, at the last trump: for the trumpet shall sound, and the dead shall be raised incorruptible, and we shall be changed" (1 Cor. 15:51,52). In addition, Christians rejoice in the promise that one day we shall behold Him and be like Him. "Beloved, now are we the sons of God, and it doth not yet appear what we shall be: but we know that, when he shall appear, we shall be like him; for we shall see him as he is" (1 John 3:2). The Christian faith is a transforming religion, and change is central to transformation. The essence of the truth becomes evident in the fact that the hymn *Amazing Grace* is one of the most popular hymns in the Christian community. Cultures sing it differently, but all sing it because "We once were lost, but now we are found, was blind but now we see." In other words, we all have experienced a change.

Third, change is necessary if the church is to be ministry-driven rather than tradition-driven. There is a tendency in many churches to be tradition-driven rather than ministry-driven. This tendency is carnal in nature and the source of our church growth problem. If we are serious about church growth we must first confess this sin before God and repent. When we redirect our spiritual priorities we will initiate change. Outreach ministry will be the result of this spiritual change. Outreach and evangelism will become not just ministries for the pastor and other leaders, but the lifestyle for the church. The church must begin thinking ministry-driven rather than tradition-driven.

For example, in the life of every church, budget time comes around periodically, for most, yearly. The tradition-driven church typically will begin the process by determining the current level of contributions. This figure will determine the bottom line for the new budget. The only other discussion then will be who gets what within the boundaries of the bottom line (current contributions). Most of the decision-making about who gets what will be determined by survival goals such as a new roof and general caretaking goals that minister to the current congregation rather than reaching out in faith, creatively and innovatively, to other people. The church that sets her budget using this approach perpetuates and preserves the status quo and is, therefore, tradition-driven rather than ministry-driven.

On the other hand, a church that begins her budgeting process by asking ministry leaders to creatively, innovatively, and prayerfully determine how the church through their leadership and ministry can best reach new generations and other lost people is ministry-driven. In this approach, the bottom line is determined by prayerfully summing the requests and believing that God will bless their faithful efforts to do His purpose. A church that approaches the budget process in the above manner is ministry-driven and thereby creates an environment for change. The tradition-driven approach gives credence and sanctions to the status quo at the pivotal point of planning; the ministry-driven approach requires faith and demonstrates a willingness to change.

What Needs Changing

The next area of discussion concerning initiating change deals with the question, "What needs changing?" or "What needs changing most?" The answer to these questions represent the basic framework for the remaining chapters in this book. Schaller lists a host of things that need changing from nearly A to Z. He admits it is an incomplete list.

A. Church music
B. The use of drama in worship
C. New channels of communication in preaching
D. An expansion in the number of off-street parking spaces
E. An improvement in the quality of the nursery
F. Changing the focus in advertising from messages from the producer of services to addressing the religious and personal needs of people
G. More weekday programming
H. A greater emphasis on adult Bible study groups
I. Offering at least two different worship experiences every weekend
J. Better training experiences for lay volunteers
K. More extensive reporting to the members about what is happening in the life of that congregation
L. A shift from a presentation to a participation approach to corporate worship
M. A non-geographical definition of tomorrow's potential constituency
N. Creating more attractive new entry points for newcomers
O. An expansion of the teaching ministry
P. Raising the overall quality of all facets of ministry
Q. Strengthening and enlarging the number and variety of face-to-face groups in that congregation
R. Strengthening local missions and outreach
S. Enlarging the ministries with families with young children
T. Welcoming adults who were reared in a different religious tradition, and

U.   Raising the level of Member contributions in order to
pay for all this.[16]

These changes require either a change in believers' hearts, or
there must be changed forms of church governance that do not
"muzzle the ox."

<u>Changed Hearts</u>. Nothing happens until hearts are changed to be
burdened for lost people. Unless churches and church members are
willing to come under the submission of the Holy Spirit and become
convicted of the carnal sin of allowing a lost world to die and go to
hell, not much will get changed. Our problem is not a procedural
problem; it is a spiritual problem. We need hearts changed. We need
hearts regenerated. We need the church to have a heart attack for lost
people. Often the reason people are not burdened for lost people is
because they, themselves, are either not saved or do not have an appreciation of from what they are saved and unto what they are saved.
Regardless, it is a spiritual problem.

We seemingly do not understand or appreciate that death is not
final for anyone. Everybody has some form of everlasting existence.
The question is *what* and *where*? Everlasting joy with the Lord or everlasting torture in hell? The first death we experience is not final for
anyone. Saved or unsaved, people do not seem to have an appreciation of this spiritual truth. Likewise, church members do not spiritually understand that we are saved unto His workmanship. It seems
that we are very familiar with Ephesians 2:8,9 "For by grace are ye
saved through faith; and that not of yourselves: it is the gift of God:
Not of works, lest any man should boast." But we ignore Ephesians
2:10 "For we are his workmanship, created in Christ Jesus unto good
works, which God hath before ordained that we should walk in them."
We have a spiritual problem. What we need most is a heart change.

A story is told about a scholarly ivy league scientist who hy-
pothesizes that he can change a pig's characteristics through a series
of developmental processes. So he took the pig through a series of
stages that included giving the pig a bath on a regular basis, maintaining the pig's hoofs, dressing the pig, tying a bow around the
pig's neck, and letting the pig sleep in the bed and lounge in casual
attire in the living room. One day while taking the pig out on a sophisticated stroll, the pig passed a mud hole and immediately jumped
in. After several repetitions of the above, the brilliant scholar gave
up. One day an uneducated country preacher came along and asked

if he might try to bring the pig into a lifestyle of acceptable social conformity. The brilliant scientist agreed and the rough-around-the-edges, uneducated preacher took the pig away for about two weeks. The day of reckoning finally came, and both the scientist and the preacher assembled to watch to see if the pig could or could not resist the temptation of the mud hole. Much to the surprise and awe of the scientist, the pig came to the mud hole, stopped and glanced at it, turned his nose into the air and with great dignity strolled pass. The scientist was amazed. "What did you do to him?" he asked. "What developmental steps did you perform? What behavioral modification did you utilize?" The country preacher said, "None." "Well how did you do it?" The country preacher replied, "I performed surgery on his heart. I took the heart out of a sheep and put it in the pig. The pig now has a sheep's heart. I performed a heart change." If we are going to initiate the type of changes needed to grow our churches, we need a heart change.

Church Governance That Does Not "Muzzle the Ox."   Also critical to initiating change is the need for a style of church governance that will not "muzzle the ox." In the context of speaking in support of this need two times (1 Cor. 9:9 and 1 Tim. 5:18), I quote Deuteronomy 25:4, "Thou shall not muzzle the ox when he treadeth out the corn." Pastors are instruments of change. Church governance must allow them to lead. Mainline churches and others who historically govern with bureaucratic church boards must change if church growth according to God's will is going to occur.

The church is not an organization. Rather, the church is an organism. One of the central characteristics of an organization is rigid structure and bureaucracy (red tape). One of the central characteristics of an organism is spontaneity. The church should be allowed to grow spontaneously. A scripturally-based style of governance should be established that will create an environment for growth. Historically, church boards have fostered organizational bureaucracy, though this is not always true. Regardless, deacons, trustees, members and others who have historically governed churches through boards must become servant leaders rather than church officers. Servant leaders that are ministry-driven operate in a mode that accepts changes. Church officers tend to be tradition-driven and operate in a maintenance mode. Churches that grow most have overcome the church board organizational syndrome.

How Do We Best Implement Change

This brings us to the final question relative to initiating change, i.e. "How do we best implement change?" Change is best implemented through leadership and the creation of an environment conducive to change.

I am often called on to conduct church growth workshops and seminars at churches across this country. Recently, I was asked to conduct a Sunday School and Church Growth Workshop in Pittsburgh. It was during the snow storm of '96. I, quite frankly, wanted to cancel. Most airports were closed, but Pittsburgh had one runway open. The pastor refused to cancel the workshop if I could get there. The pastor possessed a leadership quality conducive to church growth, a sense of urgency. After spending several days with him, I realized he had other leadership skills that are needed for church growth. This church is growing and will continue to grow under his leadership. Other times, I have visited churches where the leadership necessary for church growth is simply not there. Leadership makes the difference. Effective leadership can initiate change.

Dr. John Sullivan of the Home Mission Board of the Southern Baptist Convention stated at a church growth conference in Ft. Mill, SC: "(1) What makes leaders effective is their ability to mobilize supporters of the vision. (2) Leadership does not exist within a person, it resides in the relationship between persons. (3) Leadership is never satisfied with maintaining things as they are. Change managers formulate a vision that gives direction to the hopes and desires of others. Integrity and courage are essential. Change managers need the power to advance their idea by enlisting and involving people as well as influencing people to invest their own time, energy and resources in realizing the vision."[17]

Leaders must be anointed to carry out this task. The charge starts with the leadership. Leadership must be continually anointed by and filled with the Holy Spirit to be able to boldly, yet gently and in love, initiate change. Leaders should also become thoroughly familiar with the phenomenon of change and group dynamics. Psychology and the behavioral sciences can be helpful. But the anointing must be present. Leaders must be God-led and Holy Ghost-filled to initiate change and create an environment where change is accepted. To be an agent of change, a leader must take the gifts and resources provided by God and focus them on the task assigned by God. Anointed leaders are not afraid to take risks. Others go no farther than they believe their human strengths will allow them to venture. Effective leadership has learned the power of "dissatisfied satisfaction." Effective leaders are grateful for what God has done and are aware of what God is doing as well. They are aware that God is leading them to do something different and better.

Leadership is about change. As someone has stated, "It is important to remember that we cannot become what we need to become by remaining what we are." Also, as I so often say, "Doing the same thing over and over again and expecting different results is dumb." Thus, leadership must strive to create an environment that is conducive to change. The ability to change must become a value. It must become a Christian trait. It must become a lifestyle. Change must become so much of the norm that a church could boast that the only constant we have is change. Thus, the general congregation expects change because they realize it is necessary to do God's will. This can only happen when they learn to first trust God and then to trust God's leaders.

The major reason laity resists change is they have a strong desire to control the church. This is because they do not trust. They do not trust God and they do not trust the leadership. With God's help, the anointed leader can overcome resistance and initiate the change that is absolutely necessary for church growth. If you are faithful over this one thing, the church will have the necessary basis for growth.

In Summary

The ability to initiate change is essential for the implementation of any non-traditional principle necessary to promote church growth. In a changing society change in the church is inevitable. In addition, the Christian faith is grounded in transformation (changed lives). The need for change and the reason people require change have been discussed. In addition, these questions were addressed: "Why change?" "What needs changing?" "What needs changing most?" "How is change best implemented?"

The creation of an environment conducive to change is necessary to initiate change. The key to initiating change is effective leadership. If the church is to grow, pastors, the church, and her leadership should focus their time and energy on initiating change.

Chapter 4

Prioritize Expressive Praise and Praying in Faith

If the church and her leadership would make expressive praise and praying in faith priorities, the church will grow. Notice I did not say praise; I said "expressive praise." Praise by definition demands some form of expression. Notice I did not say just pray. I said pray in faith. If we are going to be obedient to the scripture, we must not just pray, but we must pray in faith.

In the New Testament God clearly states His will for the believer regarding praise and prayer. In 1 Thessalonians, Chapter 5 He states, "rejoice evermore" (vs 16); "Pray without ceasing" (vs 17); "Quench not the Spirit" (vs 19); and "In every thing give thanks: for this is the will of God in Christ Jesus concerning you" (vs 18). In the model prayer, Jesus taught us to pray, "Hallowed (holy) be thy name". Praise is an element of prayer, and prayer may certainly be a part of any praise. While it is true that praise and prayer are related, they demand separate attention.

Expressive Praise

If I were asked what is the one area in the life of most mainline Christian churches that needs a major change, I would say it is in the area of expressive praise. Surprisingly, this is the one area that is avoided in the research of church growth authors. It is likewise the most protected area of ownership for the mainline church laity. A common statement made by church growth consultants is that worship should be culturally relevant. This is an undeniable statement. While this is true, it provides an excuse for our carnal pride that denies God the praise He asks for in the scripture and deserves due to His goodness.

Unfortunately, we equate worship style with expressive praise. It is not my intention to discuss worship styles that are culturally or geographically specific. Praise, however, is not culturally specific. Praise is scripturally based. Worship, at least the order of Sunday morning worship, may be culturally specific. Notice, I said Sunday morning worship service order. Genuine worship defies order. "God is a Spirit: and they that worship him must worship him in spirit and in truth" (John 4:24). Worship comes from the word *worth* or *worthy*. To worship God in spirit and truth, we must spiritually understand our unworthiness as compared to His worthiness. Pure worship requires us to continuously be before God in a spiritual posture of submission (physically demonstrated as bowed down, hands up, etc.); concentrating only on Him, and praising Him in adoration and thanksgiving for who He is and what He has done. Very few, if any, of us really participate in worship in its purest form during the Sunday morning service. Therefore, on Sunday morning we gather to worship and have a predetermined order of worship. I am not suggesting a move toward a pure form of worship during the 11 o'clock Sunday morning service. What I am suggesting is an intentional move toward a demonstrative love for God in worship through the avenue of expressive praise. To be expressive means to participate deliberately or emotionally in any of the forms of biblical praise, such as kneeling, raising hands, clapping, crying, and vocal affirmations of the goodness of God. Notice, I included crying. Tears of joy, adoration, or conviction are a very acceptable form of praise. "And stood at his feet behind him weeping, and began to wash his feet with tears, and did wipe them with the hairs of her head, and kissed his feet, and anointed them with the ointment" (Luke 7:38).

The Meaning, Forms, and Scope of Expressive Praise

According to Jack Taylor in his book *The Hallelujah Factor*, praise may be (1) vocal, "My mouth shall speak the praise of the Lord" (Ps 145:21); (2) audible, such as the clapping of hands, "O clap your hands, all ye people" (Ps 47:1), or as Psalm 150 exhorts us, we should praise the Lord with instruments; (3) visual expressions such as lifting of hands, "I will lift up my hands in thy name" (Ps 63:4); or (4) dancing, "Let them praise his name in the dance" (Ps. 149:3). Praise is not an option for the believer. According to Revelation 4:11 we were created for His pleasure. Taylor offers the following working definition of praise that fits my description of expressive praise, "Praise is adoration of God that is vocal, audible, or visible (any one or all of these at a time.)"[18]

A word of caution. Praise should not be confused with emotions. A church could be a very emotional church and not be participating in true praise. This type of church will not possess the transforming power derived from praise. Praise may lead to emotions, but praise is not emotion. Real transforming praise is a deliberate act of a believer. It is born out of the love for God and His word and a desire to be obedient to His will to praise Him.

Worship, regardless of culture, denomination or style, is God's party. God is the audience, not us. God is the one to satisfy, not us. God is the one to be blessed, not us. God is the subject of our worship, not us. God is the one who desires a gift of praise to be brought to His party (worship). Our circumstances or particular situations do not determine whether we are to praise God or not. Even if we do not feel like praising God, we are to bring Him a sacrifice of praise. "By him therefore let us offer the sacrifice of praise to God continually, that is, the fruit of our lips giving thanks to his name." (Heb.13:15).

Praise must become a priority for the church that desires to grow. There is power in praise. Many believers know and have experienced the power of prayer. The Bible says much about the power of prayer, and bookstore shelves are filled with one meditation book after another about the power of prayer. However, although the Bible says much about the power of praise, man has said little and practiced even less. It is without question a jewel to be discovered or rediscovered by mainline churches. It has been suggested, and I concur, that Satan has stolen praise from the church. There is power in praise. There is victory in praise. Praise gives the believer home court advantage against the evil one because God resides in praise. "But thou art holy, O thou that inhabitest the praises of Israel."(Ps 22:3).

Of the many functions of praise, God gave praise as a weapon to fight the devil and his angels."Let the high praises of God be in their mouth, and a two edged sword in their hand; To execute vengeance upon the heathen, and punishments upon the people; To bind their kings with chains, and their nobles with fetters of iron; To execute upon them the judgment written: this honour have all his saints. Praise ye the LORD" (Ps 149:6-9).

However, the enemy stole the weapon. The effect is that the church has become fearful and resistant to biblical praise. Praise must become a priority item on the list of things to change. A.W. Tozer refers to this lost weapon of the church in his book *Worship—The Missing Jewel of the Church* when he writes, "The crown jewels of the church have been stolen. The old ship, the church, has been the victim of piracy on the high seas of time. The devil has stolen praise."[19]

Nevertheless, God cannot and will not be defeated. There is a move around the world to restore praise into the life of the church and her people. When I travel across this country observing growing churches, the praise factor is there. It is often called by different names such as celebration in praise, praise service, spiritual "happy hour", church alive, the excited church, and others. Non-growing churches need to wake up and smell the coffee. "God is restoring praise to the body of Christ all over the world."[20] If you are faithful over a few things God will grow the church. Making praise a priority is one of those few things.

Praise Prioritized—How?

How do you prioritize praise? People are moved to praise through the preached and taught word of God, the behavior of the leadership concerning praise, and opportunities provided to practice and participate in praise. People are not led to praise through fussing at, bashing, and attempts to embarrass them. Pastors and leaders who use the pulpit to talk down to people about their inability to praise or clap their hands, shout, bow down, and/or say "amen" are missing the boat. Biblical truth sets people free. "And ye shall know the truth, and the truth shall make you free."(John 8:32). People are moved from self-pride to love of God through the anointed preaching and teaching of biblical truths concerning praise. People are transformed from fear to faith by the working of the Holy Spirit in them by hearing what God has to say about praise in His word. The Bible says, "...and how shall they hear without a preacher?" (Rom 10:14). The taught word and the preached word are instruments of change. It is difficult to distinguish preaching from teaching. Both are needed. However, God's word must be proclaimed from the pulpit concerning the biblical and spiritual truth about praise for change to be most effective. To be most effective, God's word concerning praise must penetrate the congregation. Praise revival, praise seminars, and Sunday School lessons on praise are but a few of the modes that can be utilized to penetrate the hearts of the believers.

The following is a summary of a word study in Hebrew on praise that has proven to be effective.

Hallal: "to laud, boast, rave, to celebrate"— It is used approximately one hundred times in the Old Testament.

Yadah: "to worship with extended hands, to throw out the hands" — It is used over ninety times in the Old Testament. (Yad means "hand.")

Barak: "to bless, to declare God the origin of power for success, prosperity, and fertility"—It is used approximately seventy times in the Old Testament as praise to God.

Tehillah: "to sing or laud"—It is derived from *hallal* and is generally accepted to mean "the singing of *hallals*." It is used over fifty times in the Old Testament.

Zamar: "to pluck the strings of an instrument, to praise with song"—It is used almost exclusively in the Psalms and occurs approximately forty times in the Old Testament.

Todah: "to extend the hands in thanksgiving, a thank-offering" —It is used only a few times when translated "praise" but occurs many other times in connection with thanksgiving.

Shabach (Shebach): "to commend, address in a loud tone, to shout"—This is the exclamatory form of praise in a special sense and is found only about seven times in the Old Testament. It is interesting, however, to note that other words for "shout" are used in connection with the exercise of praise.[21]

Another way to prioritize praise is through the behavior of the pastor and leadership. One of the presuppositions of initiating change is that leadership makes the difference, and the pastor is the catalyst. The congregation and members should never be asked to do what the leaders do not or will not do. I have noticed that pastors, deacons, and other officers sit dignified and conservatively while the congregation attempts to praise God. The message conveyed is that praise is not a priority. If a congregation is in its embryonic stage of prioritizing praise, it would be most effective if the pastor would lead the praise. When the leaders of the church, especially the male leaders of the church, begin to praise God according to His will, a transforming power will come over the church as never before.

Yet another way to prioritize praise in the hearts of believers is by creating opportunities for participation. One may learn what to do by studying and reading, but one learns how to do by participating. In many churches there is limited opportunity for the congregation to participate in praise because the pastor and the choir dominate the worship. In prioritizing praise, time must be planned and orchestrated just as everything else is in preparing for the worship service. Singing remains the best channel of participation. Singing is God ordained, and every believer has a song in his/her heart. God blesses praise singing because it is God's will. "Make a joyful noise unto the Lord, all the earth: make a loud noise, and rejoice, and sing praise" (Ps 98:4). God did not say make a beautiful noise; He said make a joyful noise. Every believer has this capacity.

Growing congregations are singing congregations. To effectively promote praise, praise songs must be sung. Praise music has a distinction. Praise music always has God as the recipient of the song. Praise music directs blessings to God. Remember, worship is God's party. God is the audience. We are the participants. Praise music focuses the hearts of the singer on adoration directed to God. The focus of singing is toward God as a demonstrative display of our love for Him.

Traditional hymns, anthems, and spirituals that possess valuable theology lead the singers to sing about God, but seldom to God. In general people do not learn to love God by singing about Him. They learn to love God more by singing to Him. They learn about God by singing about God, but a deeper relationship with Him is formed by singing to Him.

Praise music communicates to God like prayer. That is why praise must even be a part of prayer and prayer is a part of praise. Jesus taught us to praise before we petition Him:

"Our Father which art in heaven, Hallowed be thy name. Thy kingdom come. Thy will be done in earth, as it is in heaven. Give us this day our daily bread. And forgive us our debts, as we forgive our debtors. And lead us not into temptation, but deliver us from evil: For thine is the kingdom, and the power, and the glory, for ever. Amen." (Matt 6:9-13).

There are five expressions of praise before one petition. The Lord's Prayer opens in praise and closes in praise. Praise music often recites God's words back to Him from scripture. For example, musicians have Psalm 47:1 put to melody; "Clap your hands, all ye people; shout unto God with the voice of triumph." Manifold results are gained from singing scripture. First, we learn scripture through repetition in song. Second, we learn God's will relative to a form of praise (clap your hands). Third, we do God's will by clapping our hands while we sing. Fourth, we please God by singing His words back to Him. Remember we were created for His pleasure "Thou art worthy, O Lord, to receive glory and honour and power: for thou hast created all things, and for thy pleasure they are and were created" (Rev 4:11).

Churches and pastors that desire to be a part of God's movement must join in with Him and what He is doing. God is restoring praise in the hearts of His people, whether we like it or not. Jack Taylor writes,

> It is happening! It is a work of God! No one can stop it! It has been a long time in coming. The drought has been lengthy and wearisome, but the sounds of the abundance of rain are beginning to be heard.
>
> Praise the Lord for groups springing up everywhere who seem to have led out in praise. It has been easier for them since they had no precedents to which to adhere. We may not agree on all points of doctrine, but all who know the Lord are happy to agree on the happy fact that our Lord is worthy to be praised.[22]

Churches that are faithful in their prioritizing of praise will be blessed by joining God in what He is doing.

Praying in Faith

Part two of this chapter centers on prioritizing praying in faith. As mentioned earlier, prayer and praise are interrelated but need to be discussed separately. Both praise and prayer must be prioritized because they both connect man to God in communication. Praise primarily communicates love, whereas in prayer, we are allowed to petition. Both communicate to God, therefore must be listed among the few things we must be faithful in doing if we want our churches to grow.

More has been written about the power of prayer than the power of praise. We have implied a distinction between just praying and praying in faith. Whereas praise is the key that unlocks the door for prayer, praying in faith is the catalyst that unleashes the power. In my church growth journey, two peak experiences that helped me most involved praying in faith. A peak experience is what existentialists call an episode that has indelible learning qualities. The experience pricks and sticks. When you have a peak experience, you learn something forever. A peak experience is not a conversion experience, rather it is a learning experience.

<u>The Entree—Peak Experiences</u>. The first peak experience on my church journey sprang from a question I heard a preacher ask. The question was, "What are you doing in your life, or in the life of your church, that you couldn't do without the filling of the Holy Spirit?" Upon careful examination my answer was, "Nothing." All that I was doing I could do without the filling of the Holy Spirit. I was doing absolutely nothing that needed the supernatural filling of the Holy Spirit to accomplish. I was further confronted and convicted through the scripture that says, "Wherefore be ye not unwise, but understanding what the will of the Lord is. And be not drunk with wine, wherein is excess; but be filled with the Spirit" (Eph 5:17-18).

After learning to pray in faith, I was able to overcome my backslidden posture and be filled with the Spirit. The scripture says that it is God's will for each and every Christian to be filled with the Spirit. Theologically, I understand and have always understood that when I was saved, I received not only the Holy Spirit, but the whole of the Holy Spirit; but what I did not understand was that being filled is not a one time event. The verb has a present, plural and imperative meaning. All of us (none excluded) must be continually filled with the Holy Spirit. Like all of God's commandments, this is not a divine suggestion. God is not and has never been in the suggestion business. This is God's will, that we be filled in our going—in other words, be filled in our carrying out of The Great Commission, be filled in our building of His Kingdom, be filled in the process of evangelism and church growth. The fact is, the only way we can effectively grow churches is with the supernatural power of the Holy Spirit. The question is, "How can one be continually filled?" The answer is found in the priorities discussed in this chapter, i.e., to be in submissive obedience to expressive praise and praying in faith.

We church leaders dare not try to initiate change in our traditional churches without praying in faith. Change requires supernatural power. We must lead our church in ministry opportunities that demand the supernatural filling and anointing of the Holy Spirit.

The task of going into deep and dangerous territory to witness for God provides such an opportunity. Being scared and afraid is a valid yardstick for determining supernatural need. If we are afraid to go, we need power from on high. We need visions for our churches that are so big that we realize they cannot be accomplished without God. There is only one way to do things that seem impossible to man, and that is through the supernatural power that results from praying in faith. If Jesus himself knew and felt the need to pray for empowerment, certainly so should we. Remember, Jesus prayed, and he made prayer a priority.

My second peak experience took place in a familiar discipleship course, MasterLife. One of the first teaching illustrations in the course is called the Disciple's Cross. The presentation begins by drawing a cross and placing four major roles of a disciple in the four extensions created by the vertical and horizonal lines that form the cross. One of the major discipleship roles is praying in faith. The other three are (1) living in the word, (2) witnessing to the world, and (3) fellowshiping with the believer. Most Christians have at least one identifiable area of weakness. I realized my weakness was praying in faith. Once convicted, I made a commitment to growth to overcome my weakness in the area of praying in faith. Likewise, if pastors and church leaders would come under the conviction that the reason their church is not growing is due to a spiritual problem, barriers to real true commitment could be overcome.

The Meaning. Praying in faith is praying according to the will of God. It involves not only believing that God answers prayer, but behaving as though God has already answered prayer. Praying in faith empowers the church and the believer to do things they could not do with human resources alone. I am convinced that though our prayer altar call on Sunday morning may be with great fervor, and often loud, faith that God really is going to answer our prayer is not exhibited in our behavior. Often we pray because it causes us to feel better. And that is alright. We espouse the proposition that you cannot pray and worry at the same time. And that is true. We believe that we should do as the songwriter penned, "Bring your burden to the Lord and leave it there." Or as another wrote, "I feel better, so much better, since I laid my burden down." All of the above are good, fine, and dandy, but praying in faith goes beyond just "feel better after praying" messages. Praying in faith means getting up from a bowed down prayer posture with the power to put arms and legs on the prayer and proceed, knowing that God has gone before you. That is the kind of praying we need to help God grow churches. Praying in faith connects us with God's plan and His power. Traditional prayer meetings are often too casual and fellowship oriented. Fellowship has an important role in church, but prayer meeting is a time to touch and agree: "Again I say unto you, That if two of you shall agree on earth as touching any thing that they shall ask, it shall be done for them of my Father which is in heaven" (Matt 18:19).

We act as if that scripture has been set in the concrete of history, never to be transferred to our daily contemporary living. Amazingly, we believe in the God of history, but not the Living God. Praying in faith transfers the God of Abraham, Isaac and Jacob into the living contemporary (right now) God who is yours for the asking. God gives us the privilege to pray for everything and anything, and oftentimes we do just that; pray for everything and anything except ministry issues such as church growth. Is not church growth important? Who is praying in your church for growth? Are not lost people important? Who is praying for the lost in your church? Maybe a more convicting question might be, "What percentage of the praying time is spent praying for lost people going to hell as compared to praying for sick living saints who are preparing to die and go to heaven?" One wonders whether we really believe in the reality of heaven and hell. We need to pray in faith for some evangelistic church growth victories. We give lip service to the fact that prayer changes things and people. Yet we might pray for a person to be changed and continue to treat that person as if we do not believe God will change him. Do not just pray, but rather pray in faith, and you will be able to treat that person you are praying for as if he had already changed.

The biblical definition of faith gives divine sanction to praying in faith. "Now faith is the substance of things hoped for, the evidence of things not seen" (Heb 11:1). Praying in faith brings a perspective of the substance to fruition. Through praying in faith, the Spirit of God's word becomes active. Praying in faith links prayer and scripture (His word). God is a promise keeper, and he has promised us in His word that He will answer prayer. The following scriptures are God's promises concerning prayer:

"If ye abide in me, and my words abide in you, ye shall ask what ye will, and it shall be done unto you" (John 15:7).

"And whatsoever we ask, we receive of him, because we keep his commandments, and do those things that are pleasing in his sight" (1 John 3:22).

"Yet ye have not, because ye ask not" (James 4:2b).

We are a covenant people, and we have a covenant relationship with God. If He said He will do it, then He will do it, if we keep our end of the relationship. As Avery Willis, Jr., says "In the Bible, covenants between God and His people had three stages. (1) God revealed His will and made a promise; (2) The people met the conditions God laid down; and (3) the people believed God and received the blessing."[23] Scriptural illustrations can be found throughout the Bible: Gen. 17:9-16,23; Jer.34:13-16; Luke 19:12-15,21,22; John 9:6,7.

The Steps. We have a prayer covenant with God, and God always does His part. We too, must do our part. We must learn to pray in faith. MasterLife Discipleship Training offers six steps to praying in faith:

Step One: Abide in Christ
Step Two: Abide in the Word
Step Three: Allow the Holy Spirit to Lead
Step Four: Ask According to God's Will
Step Five: Accept God's Will in Faith
Step Six: Act on the Basis of God's Word to You[24]

Praying in Faith Prioritized...How?

The same requirement to prioritize expressive praise holds true for prioritizing praying in faith. To begin with, leadership makes the difference, and the pastor, as always, is the sparkplug. Leaders must behave in a faith manner. This can be felt and seen in their decision-making processes and in how they live their personal lives. Budgets made based on last year's income illustrate leadership that cares little about living by faith and certainly does not possess the grace of praying in faith. Leaders who lead the church to take risks appear as men and women who pray in faith. Teach the church to pray in faith for personal victories in their lives. Demonstrate praying in faith from the pulpit. I often tell the congregation that I am praying in faith for a certain thing, and I will literally take a victory lap (a run around the pews in the church) because I know God is going to do it. Leaders must educate the congregation on praying in faith. The Bible study on praying in faith in the MasterLife Discipleship Training Manual is excellent. In general, it advocates organizing the church to pray. Here are a few ideas.

1. Organize prayer groups through Sunday School classes or other cell groups
2. Use prayer chains.
3. Use days of prayer and fasting.
4. Develop a system of prayer partners.
5. Have regularly scheduled days for concerts of prayer.
6. Develop a prayer chapel that is accessible around the clock.
7. Have a prayer hotline [25]

The prioritizing of praying in faith is most important if we want God to grow the church and bless our labor. Prioritizing praise and prayer leads to discipleship and being filled with the Holy Spirit. Disciples are what the church is called to make in the first place. "Go ye therefore, and teach all nations," (Matt. 28:19a). If you produce disciplined learners and followers of Christ the church will not only grow numerically but also spiritually. *Real spiritual growth will always produce numerical growth.*

As discussed, expressive praise and praying in faith assure the continuous filling of the Holy Spirit (Eph. 5:18b). Being filled with the Holy Spirit is necessary for authentic church growth. When we are filled with the Holy Spirit, we do what we should as we are going, and we do what the Bible says is the will of God.

The Great Commission clearly says that we are to make disciples as we are going. The pastor is busy and always on the go. The church and her members are always on the go. This book is about time focus and prioritizing our tasks as we go so that we can be faithful over a few things. Expressive praise and praying in faith provide the avenue for keeping this commandment.

The Bible records God's will for us in Ephesians 5:17b and 18, "...but understanding what the will of the Lord is. And be not drunk with wine, wherein is excess; but be filled with the Spirit." Notice that God categorizes not being drunk with being filled with the Holy Spirit. The inference is that not being filled with the Holy Spirit is as carnal as being drunk with wine. It is God's will that we be continuously filled. Prioritizing expressive praise and praying in faith are God-given ways of assuring that God's will will be done. Thus, the church will grow. Again, spiritual growth always produces numerical growth. Such is the will of God, "if, thou hast been faithful over a few things, I will make thee ruler over many things:" (Matt. 25:21).

In Summary
A distinction is made between expressive praise and a casual use of the term praise. Likewise, a distinction is made between casual routine prayer and praying in faith. Praise and prayer are interrelated. Both expressive praise and praying in faith are critical to church growth. Expressive praise and praying in faith have been explored and analyzed from a biblical perspective. The role of the Holy Spirit was examined relative to praying in faith and church growth, and suggestions on how to incorporate expressive praise and praying in faith into the local church were offered.

Chapter 5

Orchestrate Intentional Evangelism and Outreach Ministries

The Necessity

If the church is going to be faithful to her calling to "Go," evangelism must become the lifestyle of the church. Most churches recognize and give lip service to The Great Commission, "Go ye therefore, and teach all nations, baptizing them in the name of the Father, and of the Son, and of the Holy Ghost: Teaching them to observe all things whatsoever I have commanded you: and, lo, I am with you alway, even unto the end of the world. Amen."(Matt 28:19-20). Few churches consider the command worthy of an all out effort for the entire congregation. After all, the church has other functions: worship, discipleship, and fellowship. All are important to the growing church. However, the pastors and church leaders that want their churches to grow must make an intentional effort to make evangelism and outreach ministry a major focus in the life of the church. The key word is intentional or purposeful. Effective evangelism does not just happen. There must be a purposeful endeavor. There must be a directional focus. There must be a developed atmosphere. There must be a spiritual understanding of the purposeful direction. Also, it must be the task of all believers in the local church. More often than not, the task of evangelism becomes the responsibility of the pastor, minister of evangelism, Sunday School outreach director, and a faithful few who feel they have the gift of evangelism. The task is not just for those who have a special calling; the call is for all believers. God's agenda is not worship, although we were created for that purpose (Rev 4:11), or even fellowship. His prime reason for coming was to seek and save the lost (Luke 19:10). If we are going to be faithful followers, we must intentionally make His agenda ours.

Evangelism must become intentional for the growing church, and it must become a lifestyle for her members. The task is not easy. Several questions need to be addressed. (1) What is the major prohibiting factor? (2) What are the biblical mandates? (3) How do you orchestrate intentional evangelism and outreach ministries? (4) Are there specific approaches that have proven better than others?

Major Prohibiting Factor

A church that does not purposefully evangelize and develop outreach ministries does not measure up to God's plumb line for the church. Amos speaks to us about the plumb line (Amos 7:8). The plumb line is an object that builders use to measure the straightness of a wall. God uses it as an object lesson for the church to determine whether or not we are on course. Are we straight and doing what we ought to do? The major prohibiting factor is that churches do not view evangelism as their major reason for existing. We ought to have evangelism as a primary purpose. The church does not measure up well against the plumb line when the church puts other activities and functions ahead of evangelism. For example, fellowship is a major function of the church. One of the benefits of fellowship is drawing strength from one another to go back into the field of evangelism.

The Need to Break the Huddle. We must break the huddle of fellowship and carry out the plan. Too often the church never really breaks the huddle. In football the team huddles to get the play from the quarterback. After receiving the plan they break the huddle and run the play. The church is guilty of staying in the huddle. The church needs to break the huddle. When Jesus took Peter, James and John on the mountain top where He was transfigured and shown in all His glory, there was a tremendous temptation to huddle there forever! "Then answered Peter, and said unto Jesus, Lord, it is good for us to be here: if thou wilt, *let us make here three tabernacles* [huddle]; one for thee, and one for Moses, and one for Elias." (Matt 17:4). But Jesus reminded them that there was work to do in the valley. We can not fellowship forever when God wants to use us to seek and save others.

There is another pertinent spiritual lesson to be learned from the transfiguration narrative. God does not provide us mountain top experiences without a purpose. We are inspired for a purpose. When worship ends, service begins. The cross is not only vertical, it is also horizontal. It reaches up and gathers power from on high and reaches down grounded in incarnate love. But it also reaches out horizontally to minister and gather in the lost and unchurched. Churches that do not have evangelism and outreach ministries as primary functions are serving only the vertical portion of the cross and are out of step with the New Testament church's calling.

The Biblical Mandate for the New Testament Church to Evangelize

The biblical call for the New Testament church to evangelize can be summed up in four areas: (1) The Invitation, (2) The Expectation, (3) The Need, and (4) The Responsibility.[26] The invitation is to fish, the expectation is that we will go, the need is great, and the responsibility is ours.

The Invitation to Fish (The Great Growth Commission). In Luke 5, the invitation is given in what I have come to know as the "Great Growth Commission." Jesus found a group of fishermen away from their boats washing their nets. Jesus summoned them into the boats and proceeded to teach them about fishing. They learned by His example that they must be *in* the boat to fish. Many churches are out of the boat. They are talking about fishing and going to fishing conferences, yet they are not fishing. They are washing their nets preparing to fish, but not fishing. After summoning the fishermen into the boat, Jesus instructed them to push out into the deep waters and "launch out into the deep, and let down your nets for a draught" (Luke 5:4). In this one verse, Jesus taught them to fish with a big net rather than with a pole and bait in deep waters. Deep waters and net fishing represent heterogeneous evangelism. Targeting a certain population to evangelize is a proven marketing technique, but not a biblical truth. Everything that is true is not biblical. The scripture lesson begins to conclude when the fishermen step for a moment out of their carnal thinking and, in obedience to Jesus, cast their nets in deep water. The results were frightening. The gathering was so plentiful that it broke the net and other fishermen (churches) were invited to share in the results. Peter was awestruck. He fell on his knees before a Holy God and confessed his sinfulness. Then the invitation was given, "Fear not; from henceforth thou shalt catch men" (Luke 5:10). The majority of churches today need to be brought to their knees and confess their spiritual problems that are prohibiting church growth and then, in obedience, be faithful over a few things that will fulfill God's purpose to seek and save.

The invitation is to net fish in deep water. We are to be fishermen of men *in* the boat, with Jesus as the captain and the Holy Spirit as the pilot. Intentional, purposeful fishing is a must. Remember the invitation is not to talk about fishing (washing nets); the invitation is to fish. Prayerfully, the following contemporary parable written by John M. Drescher will lead to an acceptance of the invitation to do intentional fishing for men.

Now it came to pass that a group existed who called themselves fishermen. And lo, there were many fish in the waters all around. In fact, the whole area was surrounded by streams and lakes filled with fish. And the fish were hungry.

Week after week, month after month, and year after year, these who called themselves fishermen met in meetings and talked about their call to fish, the abundance of fish, and how they might go about fishing. Year after year they carefully defined what fishing means, defended fishing as an occupation, and declared that fishing is always to be a primary task of fisherman.

Continually, they searched for new and better methods of fishing and for new and better definitions of fishing. Further they said, 'The fishing industry exists by fishing as fire exists by burning.' They loved slogans such as 'Fishing is the task of every fisherman.' They sponsored special meetings called 'Fishermen's Campaigns' and 'The Month for Fishermen to Fish.' They sponsored costly nationwide and worldwide congresses to discuss fishing and to promote fishing and hear about all the ways of fishing such as the new fishing equipment, fish calls, and whether any new bait had been discovered.

These fishermen built large, beautiful buildings called 'Fishing Headquarters.' The plea was that everyone should be a fisherman and every fisherman should fish. One thing they didn't do, however: The didn't fish.

In addition to meeting regularly, they organized a board to send out fishermen to other places where there were many fish. The board hired staffs and appointed committees and held many meetings to define fishing, to defend fishing, and to decide what new streams should be thought about. But the staff and committee members did not fish.

Large, elaborate, and expensive training centers were built whose original and primary purpose was to teach fishermen how to fish. Over the years courses were offered on the needs of fish, the nature of fish, where to find fish, the psychological reactions of fish, and how to approach and feed fish. Those who taught had doctorates in fishology, but the teachers did not fish. They only taught fishing. Year after year, after tedious training, many were graduated and were given fishing licenses. They were sent to do full-time fishing, some to distant waters which were filled with fish.

Many who felt the call to be fishermen responded. They were commissioned and sent to fish. But like fishermen back home, they never fished. Like the fishermen back home, they engaged in all kinds of other occupations. They built power plants to pump water for fish and tractors to plow new waterways. They made all kinds of equipment to travel here and there to look at fish hatcheries. Some also said that they wanted to be part of the fishing party, but they felt called to furnish fishing equipment. Others felt their job was to relate to the fish in a good way so the fish would know the difference between good and bad fishermen. Others felt that simply letting the fish know they were nice, land-loving neighbors and how loving and kind they were was enough.

After one stirring meeting on 'The Necessity for Fishing,' one young fellow left the meeting and went fishing. The next day he reported that he had caught two outstanding fish. He was honored for his excellent catch and scheduled to visit all the big meetings possible to tell how he did it. So he quit his fishing in order to have time to tell about the experience to the other fishermen. He was also placed on the Fishermen's General Board as a person having considerable experience.

Now it is true that many of the fishermen sacrificed and put up with all kinds of difficulties. Some lived near the water and bore the smell of dead fish every day. They received the ridicule of some who made fun of their fishermen's clubs and the fact that they claimed to be fishermen yet never fished. They wondered about those who felt it was of little use to attend the weekly meetings to talk about fishing. After all, were they not following the Master who said, 'Follow me, and I will make you fishers of men'?

Imagine how hurt some were when one day a person suggested that those who don't catch fish were really not fishermen, no matter how much they claimed to be. Yet it did sound correct. Is a person a fisherman if, year after year, he never catches a fish? Is one following if he isn't fishing?[27]

A word of caution at this point about fishing. Fish that are not discipled will spoil and smell. Intentional evangelism must be balanced with monitored discipleship. Discipleship was discussed earlier in Chapter Two.

The Expectation. The expectation is that we will fish. The invitation is to fish. The command is to "Go ye therefore, and teach all nations, baptizing them in the name of the Father, and of the Son, and of the Holy Ghost: Teaching them to observe all things whatsoever I have commanded you: and, lo, I am with you alway, even unto the end of the world. Amen."(Matt. 28:19-20). The expectation for the Christian army is to "Go"; and while we are going, do these things, but "Go." Therefore, it must be understood that while we are fishing we will disciple. As a matter of fact evangelism is but the beginning of discipleship. The first order for the disciple is to go fish for men. However, we will discuss discipleship separately. It has been correctly stated that The Great Commission is not a suggestion. Most church members do not think of Matthew 28:19-20 as a commandment. Many church members feel that what is not one of the Mosaic Ten Commandments is merely a suggestion. In a recent survey, "nine out of ten pastors indicated that the primary concern of the church is to reach the unsaved and unchurched. In response to the same question, eight out of ten church members felt that the primary ministry of the church was to meet the needs of the members."[28] That is spiritual narcissism or self-love. We are massaging ourselves in unholy huddles. We are our own spiritual masseurs. We have bought into the lyrics of the old song, "Just Molly and me and the baby makes three, we're happy in our blue heaven."

The church must understand that The Great Commission is not optional. There is a choice to accept or reject the invitation for salvation, but once saved, the born again believer has no option but to make disciples as he travels the Christian journey. This going must be planned, preached, and orchestrated if the church is going to grow. "Again, this is clearly a command to the believer, predicated first on Jesus' purpose. Jesus was sent. He was on a mission. He was under a commandment to reach and save a lost world. Likewise, those who are connected to Him and joined with Him by the power of the Holy Spirit are under a commandment."[29]

The Need

A third area related to the biblical call to do intentional and purposeful evangelism is the need people have for the Lord. We should be careful how we suggest to people that God needs them. We must caution ourselves about suggesting to drug addicts and prostitutes that God needs them. I saw a church recruiting flyer that was to be distributed in the neighborhood that basically said, "God Needs You." This recruiting flyer brought to mind the Army's slogan "Uncle Sam Wants You." While this may be an attractive and magnetic marketing strategy, it lies in opposition to the biblical truth of a sovereign God. Recruiting and evangelism differ. Secular armies recruit, but the Christian army evangelizes. God really does not need us, but we need Him. We are privileged that He has chosen us to be on His team. People need the Lord. There is a void in all people that cannot be filled without a personal relationship with Christ. There is a God hole in each of us where only Jesus fits. Many try to fill this void in various ways, such as with drugs, sex, work, play, and even religion. But only a personal relationship with Christ will fill and satisfy. People without Christ in their lives are generally miserable, even though they hide behind masks such as success, fine clothes, cars, achievement, careers, and even church membership. Not only are they miserable but they are going to hell. The Bible teaches the reality of an everlasting conscious existence separated from God after the first death in hell. Not only is life everlasting but so is hell. People need the Lord because if they die outside of a personal relationship with Him, they spend eternity in hell. All people need the Lord. "For all have sinned, and come short of the glory of God;" (Rom. 3:23). We sin by nature and choice. We were born in sin and shaped in iniquity. "Behold, I was shapen in iniquity; and in sin did my mother conceive me" (Ps. 51:5). "For the wages of sin is death; but the gift of God is eternal life through Jesus Christ our Lord" (Rom 6:23). The payment for sin is death. Thank God Jesus paid it all. People need to be told this simple truth. Greg Nelson and Phil McHugh spoke well of the human predicament when they wrote the words:

> People need the Lord. People need the Lord.
> At the end of broken dreams, He's the open door.
> People need the Lord. People need the Lord.
> When will we realize, People need the Lord.[30]

Three Christian superlatives are noteworthy: (1) The greatest need of this day is for Christians who will witness for our Lord Jesus and live devoted lives for His honor and glory. (2) The greatest tragedy for a Christian would be to stand before Christ empty-handed at the judgment having lived in a world of lost sinners and never having brought one soul to Christ. (3) The greatest joy for a Christian is to be used to win another to Christ.[31]

The Responsibility. The responsibility of Christians to fulfill the mission of Christ is given to God's Dream Team—the Holy Word, the Holy Spirit, and His Holy People. It is a privilege to be a part of this fabulous Dream Team. When the United States became sick and tired of losing in Olympic basketball, it put together a group of players called the Dream Team. Surely no other team could beat this team! After all, basketball was invented in the USA, and we certainly could not allow another country to beat us in the game that originated with us and that we taught the rest of the world to play. The Olympic Dream Team won. From the formation of the world, God had a Dream Team in mind to call men and women into conviction and confession, repentance and commitment. The Holy Spirit empowers and precedes, the Word of God convicts and compels, and the Holy People seek and tell. What should God's people tell? The Good News, the Gospel, and their testimony about the saving power of Christ and how they qualified to be on the Dream Team. We should tell what Jesus has done and is doing in their lives. What an honor. What a privilege: "ye shall be witnesses" (Acts 1:8). "But ye are a chosen generation, a royal priesthood, an holy nation, a peculiar people; that ye should shew forth the praises of him who hath called you out of darkness into his marvellous light:" (1 Pet 2:9). It is our responsibility. If God saves you, you must tell somebody. If God healed or delivered you, you need to tell somebody. What God does for you in private is your responsibility to make public.

Why then has the church and her members failed to carry out their responsibility? Sadie McCalep lists six reasons why churches do not live up to their responsibility of witnessing. "First, there is a gap between cognitive (knowledge) learning and our affective (spiritual) learning. Second, people deny that God asks every Christian's help in saving a lost world. Third, the reason people fail to get involved is because they are afraid, ashamed or shy. Fourth, people fail to do outreach because many of them have a phobia of or a mental block about memorizing soul-winning scripture. Fifth, many have no burden for the lost. Sixth, many have no story to tell.[32]

Each of the reasons why we, the church, fail to carry our load of the Dream Team responsibility has some merit. For example, many people give lip service to their intellectual belief of heaven and hell, yet their behavior dictates that they really do not believe that heaven and hell are real. Our theology is inconsistent with our behavior. That is why we have no burden for the lost, not even our own family members. If we believed in our hearts that our friends and loved ones were going to burn everlastingly we would be burdened for their salvation. In the biblical narrative of the rich man in hell, he begged for the opportunity to go back home from hell to participate in witnessing to his brothers. "And he said, Nay, father Abraham: but if one went unto them from the dead [from hell], they will repent" (Luke 16:30) But Abraham said to him, "If they hear not Moses and the prophets [or my preacher in the local church], neither will they be persuaded, though one rose from the dead [come back from hell]" (Luke 16:31). Going to hell is a one way trip. There is no round trip ticket, and there is no probation or time off for good behavior. There is no route back. One cannot participate in evangelism from hell. Our burden for the lost should be as passionate as if *we* had been to hell, experienced it and come back.

Another reason church members do not participate in the witnessing task is that many discover that they have no story to tell, no testimony to share. Being a church member is such an inherent part of our American family value system that many church members have sought no personal relationship with Christ. Therefore, intentional purposeful witnessing should also target the general congregation, particularly new members. When new members are asked to share their testimony by articulating (1) how my life was before I met Jesus; (2) how I met Jesus; and (3) how my life has changed since I met Jesus, they find themselves wanting. Purposeful evangelism should also serve as a checks and balance system for current church members.

Yet another reason believers do not witness is because of fear; fear of rejection, fear of ridicule, and fear of not being able to memorize soul-winning scripture. Intentional purposeful evangelism teaches the entire congregation to share Jesus in a non-threatening way. One such learning module is "People Sharing Jesus." This module teaches believers to simply share Jesus based on their understanding of the presence of Jesus in their personal lives, the nature of God, and the nature of people. Intentional evangelism finds ways to overcome the reasons why people do not witness.

How to Orchestrate Purposeful Evangelism and Outreach Ministries

The most pertinent question that needs addressing in this chapter is, "How do you orchestrate intentional, purposeful evangelism and outreach ministries?" First, to orchestrate, you must have an orchestra conductor. The pastor is the orchestra conductor, and the congregation is the orchestra. The conductor must consider this task important. There is only so much time in the day. This is one of the few things to which the pastor must give his personal attention even if the church is blessed with a good, full-time minister of evangelism. However, a full-time minister of evangelism is one of the best investments a church can make. Regardless, the pastor should insist on all the paid staff being involved in all evangelistic events and efforts. All church job descriptions should include an evangelistic responsibility.

Preaching (Divine Persuasion). The pastor's hermeneutics should consist of a perpetual evangelistic thrust. In other words, the preaching should constantly include evangelistic truth. The preacher should preach for a decision to join Christ in the mission of seeking and saving. It is important to remember that the church growth problem is not a resource problem but rather a spiritual problem. The best solution to a spiritual problem is a steady diet of divine persuasion from God's word preached with the anointing of the Holy Spirit. Preaching evangelistic messages is a must for orchestrated intentional evangelism.

In addition to the regular preaching having an evangelistic zeal, special evangelistic revivals should be a part of the church's annual planning. Remember, revival is first for the saints and not the sinner. God gave us a formula for revival through Solomon: "If my people, which are called by my name, shall humble themselves, and pray, and seek my face, and turn from their wicked ways; then will I hear from heaven, and will forgive their sin, and will heal their land [then will I send down a revival or clean their carnality]" (2 Chr. 7:14). My people refers to the "called out". If the called out get revived then the church will grow. Revival infers that something once lived. If the people of God get right with Him we can be the salt and light He wants us to be.

Outreach Ministries

Intentional evangelism, however, should not be limited to the preached word during the worship service. As a matter of fact, intentional evangelism does not use a rifle approach. Rather, a shotgun approach is needed for the task. Intentional evangelism purposefully creates witnessing opportunities. Outreach ministries, soul-winning seminars, evangelistic events, marketing strategies— all have a role to play in an orchestrated evangelistic church. Outreach ministries serve two major functions. They create evangelistic opportunities as well as minister to the hope, hurts and needs of the community. Oftentimes only the latter is served. However, each outreach ministry should be programmed toward evangelism. For example, the church might have a recreation/athletic outreach ministry. This could easily become just a time to play ball, but orchestrate intentional evangelistic opportunities into the recreation ministry. During a game at half-time, for example, the Plan of Salvation could be offered to both players and spectators. All outreach ministry should present alternative entry doors into the Kingdom other than the traditional invitation time during the 11 o'clock service. Outreach ministries may include an academic center, a wellness center, an economic development corporation, a drug rehabilitation center/service, and others. Outreach ministries are only limited by the creative and innovative skills of the pastor and church.

The Sunday School as an Outreach Ministry. An often overlooked and underutilized outreach ministry that is generally a part of every church's regular activities is the Sunday School. The Sunday School is probably the most conducive structure in the church for the laity to be perpetually involved in evangelism. Most traditional Sunday

Schools serve as the teaching arm of the church. Intentional evangelistic churches utilize the Sunday School as the evangelistic arm of the church. Traditional mainline Sunday Schools are referred to as T.O.S.S. (Tradition-Oriented Sunday School); whereas G.O.S.S refers to the Growth Oriented Sunday School. The major aspect of a growth-oriented Sunday School is intentional evangelism. The G.O.S.S identifies and enrolls the lost and unchurched in Sunday morning Bible study. The growth oriented Sunday School is organized for growth. In growth-oriented Sunday Schools, each class is required to have an outreach leader, and each class is expected to identify prospects and make evangelistic visitations.

Witnessing Approaches

In the intentional evangelistic church, all outreach ministries and all programming possess a witnessing component. Leadership should be trained in methods and techniques of soul-winning. Ideally, everyone should be trained in at least one soul-winning approach and presentation. The church should adopt one simple approach and presentation, such as the F.I.R.E. approach, the Roman Road presentation, or the F.I.R.M approach. The F.I.R.E approach is taken from the *Continuing Witness Training*[33] curriculum which teaches the acronym F.I.R.E. (Family, Interest, Religious background, Exploratory questions) as an introduction to a witnessing opportunity. The acronym F.I.R.M. (Family, Interest, Religion, Message) is taught in the *People Sharing Jesus*[9] module. The Roman Road is an orderly presentation of the saving knowledge of Jesus Christ and is presented below:

> **Romans 3:23** For all have sinned, and come short of the glory of God.

> **Romans 6:23** For the wages of sin is death; but the gift of God is eternal life through Jesus Christ our Lord.

> **Romans 5:8** But God commendeth his love toward us, in that, while we were yet sinners, Christ died for us.

> **Romans 10:9-13** That if thou shalt confess with thy mouth the Lord Jesus, and shalt believe in thine heart that God hath raised him from the dead, thou shalt be saved. For with the heart man believeth unto righteousness; and with the mouth confession is made unto salvation. For the scrip-

ture saith, Whosoever believeth on him shall not be ashamed. For there is no difference between the Jew and the Greek: for the same Lord over all is rich unto all that call upon him. For whosoever shall call upon the name of the Lord shall be saved.

Remember that most people are fearful of a memorized scripture presentation. They are even fearful of reading scripture presentations to a lost person. The most non-threatening method is to teach the believers to share their own testimony. The believer's testimony is not argumentative. Nobody can debate with an individual about what the Lord has done in his life.

There are many simple presentations of the gospel. The intentional evangelistic church should adopt one method and expect each member to learn it. Notice, one method is adopted. All the methods are good, but one method is enough. While it is idealistic to think that every member will learn the one method, the expectation helps the church stay focused and motivated.

It is not unrealistic to expect the leadership to be trained in a more intensive evangelistic course such as Continuing Witness Training. CWT is a 13-week course that includes a study of intercessory prayer, systematic Bible study, memorization, reviewing sessions, witnessing experiences, and periods to report and evaluate witnessing experiences. While CWT and other intensive training curricula are not for everybody, the intentional evangelistic church expects the leadership to possess such training. Other curricula include WIN School, One Day Soul-Winning Workshop, and others, all available through the Home Mission Board of the Southern Baptist Convention. Again, the intentional evangelistic church should adopt one of the training courses in order to stay focused and effective. There are many methods and teaching strategies. The goal is to choose one and strive toward perfection. Remember, you do not have to do and cannot do everything, but you can do a few things well.

Marketing Strategies. Because intentional evangelism is broad enough to target different audiences, marketing strategies are also utilized. Many Christians object to marketing strategies because of their secular nature. The criticism is understandable, but remember, God judges our motives and our heart. Salvation should not be the best kept secret. There are many marketing strategies that can be used such as telemarketing, direct mailing, billboards, radio and television ads. George Barna, in his book *Marketing Your Church*, elaborates on the various strategies. Interestingly, all marketing surveys indicate that when asked, "How did you initially get to the church where you are a member?", the majority say through a friend, other member, or a relative.

Word-of-Mouth Strategies. Intentional evangelistic churches take advantage of the reality and effectiveness of word-of-mouth marketing. Time, budget resources, leadership expertise, and congregational involvement should reflect and focus on word-of-mouth strategies. Word-of-mouth strategies are not only most effective, they are less expensive. Word-of-mouth strategies are limited only by the innovativeness and creativity of the leadership. Greenforest Baptist Church created a "six pac" to pass out to each member. The six pac simply included six church business cards and six flyers describing the church to be distributed during the week. Another method used was for the congregation to mail the tracts on eternal life with Christmas cards to friends and family.

A key component in developing word-of-mouth strategies is to target new members. Realistically, the longer you have been a Christian and church member, the fewer non-Christians and unchurched people you actually know. The opposite is generally true with the new convert and new church member. The intentional evangelistic church emphasizes the need to develop word-of-mouth strategies that are designed specifically for new church members and converts.

Notice the pattern of intentional evangelism is to move from broad to narrow. We moved theologically to an understanding that the primary evangelistic problem of the church is not a resource problem, but a spiritual problem; and the most effective way to move people is through the divine persuasion of the preached word. We have moved from marketing with a shotgun approach to the narrower word-of-mouth approach, targeting new members and converts in particular. We have moved methodologically from an intensified scripture memorization to simply asking the congregation to share their testimonies with others. Orchestrated intentional evangelism is what this book is all about. The conductor has many instruments to direct, and many sections of the band need his attention. He cannot give prime time to everything, but he can be "faithful over a few things."

In Summary

The necessity for instituting intentional evangelism has been explored, analyzed, and discussed. The major prohibiting factor is that churches do not perceive evangelism as their primary reason for existing. There is a clear biblical call for the New Testament church to evangelize. The biblical call to evangelize was discussed concerning: (1) The Invitation, (2) The Expectation, (3) The Need, and (4) The Responsibility. Outreach ministry provides entry stations into the church other than the traditional invitation time (opening the doors of the church) at the end of the worship service. Strategies for implementation were discussed and include preaching with a purpose, various outreach ministries, Sunday School, witnessing presentations and approaches, marketing, and word-of-mouth strategies.

Chapter 6

Assure and Monitor Assimilation

Assimilation Defined

Assimilation is defined by Webster as "taking something in and making it a part of oneself." Assimilation in the church is that process which makes new members an accepted, valued, comfortable part of the church as perceived by themselves. The pastor of a growing church must plug this process into his busy schedule to assure that it happens. Otherwise the church becomes like a revolving door at a downtown department store with people coming in and people going out. The front door is open, and so is the back door. There is a "welcome in" mat at the front door, and oftentimes there is a perceived "welcome out" mat at the back door. Get the picture. The back gate is closed, but sheep are escaping over, under, and through the backyard fence. Assimilation has as its task to close the back door and shore up the sagging back yard fence. Hardaway says "The relationship of a member to his or her church is much like a marriage, except that the decision to break off or continue the relationship rests primarily in the hands of only one party. Using this perspective, the assimilation process can be seen as the engagement."[35]

The Process of Assimilation

The process of assimilation engages the church and the new member in the "honeymoon period." Marriage fails when the bride and bridegroom fail to communicate effectively during the honeymoon period. Marriage also fails when the marriage parties do not address the expectations of the marriage during the honeymoon period. In the process of church assimilation, the burden of responsibility falls entirely on one party, the church. The church must immediately address the expectations and needs of the newcomer or failure results and another sheep jumps the back fence. Whether or not a new member is accepted, used and valued is a one-sided verdict. The new member is the judge and jury. Often, churches try to make the judgement, but the church is in no position to do so because the church is the one being judged. The church can only monitor its effectiveness and initiate change based on the recorded data. Assimilation must be monitored. Many churches think this is a small component of church growth and, therefore, overlook it. Yet, if assimilation is not assured, evangelistic efforts will become counterproductive. It is like playing a man-to-man defense in a competitive sport. If every man effectively defends his assigned man the defense works; but if just one defender does not carry out his assignment, the opposition scores and the other effective players' efforts are wasted and become futile. When we effectively bring people in the front door and do not assure effective assimilation, the ministry of evangelism becomes counterproductive.

Assimilation is important because new members are the life sustaining blood of the body. God describes the church as a living organism. This is one of the favorite motifs of Paul when he speaks of the eye and the hand in 1 Corinthians:

> "For the body is not one member, but many. If the foot shall say, Because I am not the hand, I am not of the body; is it therefore not of the body? And if the ear shall say, Because I am not the eye, I am not of the body; is it therefore not of the body? If the whole body were an eye, where were the hearing? If the whole were hearing, where were the smelling? But now hath God set the members every one of them in the body, as it hath pleased him. And if they were all one member, where were the body? But now are they many members, yet but one body. And the eye cannot say unto the hand, I have no need of thee: nor again the head to the feet, I have no need of you" (1 Cor 12:14-21).

Each part is equally dependent on each other. In this case evangelism may be viewed as the heart, and assimilation as the blood.

Equally important, assimilation is a major part of the body's natural metabolic process. In the human body food is taken in through the mouth and through a complex process called digestion it is prepared to enter the blood stream to be carried throughout the body for nutrition and energy. But this cannot take place without one small process called assimilation or absorption. The process takes place in the small intestine through the villi that utilize little hair-like structures called cilli. Digested food is absorbed into the blood stream. What is not assimilated is passed from the body in the form of waste. I would not dare go so far as to call new members who leave the church waste, but oftentimes that is how we treat them and how we think of them. We must assure that the assimilation process works well because new members are the life-sustaining blood of the church. Pastors and churches that do not recognize this fact are working at a handicap. New members bring enthusiasm that has not been dampened by years of church controversy or conflict, an excitement for God that is yet to be tainted, and an openness to the will of God that has not yet been stifled by tradition. They also bring a knowledge of lost and unchurched persons that has not been diluted by years of associating only with born-again sanctified church members. New members know more people who are unsaved and unchurched because their more recent associations have been in that arena. The reality is that the longer you have been saved, the fewer unsaved people you know. The shorter the time span you have either been saved, churched, or committed, the more people you know who are in your identical predicament. New members, therefore, are the life sustaining blood of the growing church. Pastors and leaders need to assure, protect, and nurture new members. Oftentimes this is risky on the part of the pastor because he will be accused of catering to new members by existing members who fear change. Assimilation is so important that the pastor must take this risk. This is without question one of the few things the pastor must do. Of course, like the other seven critical things the pastor must do, he should not and cannot do it all himself. But a few things demand his prime time attention. Prime time attention may or may not mean being actively involved in the process of assimilation. Depending on the size of the church and some other factors, the pastor should teach or conduct the new member orientation process.

The best avenue to solve and assure the assimilation process is to discover why people join church in the first place. With all our concentration on programming and recruiting, marketing studies show that 90 percent of people come to a particular church because they were invited by a friend or associate. Newcomers and even lost persons expect a church to be friendly. Our society's value system has taught us to expect a church to act friendly. Therefore those who come are expecting to find a friend. No, they do not come looking for

a friendly church; they come looking for a friend. Forming friendships and personal relationships are the key to effective assimilation.
From the long-running popular sitcom "Cheers," a classic line in the
musical theme is, "I want to go where everybody knows my name."
The setting is a pub where the same crowd comes to drink beer. But
the people who sit on a barstool evening after evening are not there
because they like beer, but because it is a place where everybody
knows their name. That is what assimilation is all about, being in a
place that accepts you and makes you feel wanted. Granted, some
people join churches for the wrong reasons, such as for business (ma-
terialistic) reasons. There is not much we can do about that except try
to help them mature. However, our assimilation efforts should be on
those who come with a spiritual need that can only be filled by God
with the help of the people of God.

Often churches perceive themselves as friendly when really they
are not. They are friendly to each other but not friendly to outsiders,
and make no mistake, new members are outsiders. This can be viewed
as a sociological dynamic. According to the science of "group dynamics" all groups form boundary lines. Boundaries can sometimes
be semi-permeable and sometimes non-permeable and extremely
difficult to penetrate. In any social group there is always the phenomenon of "we" and "they." On one Sunday when the church I
pastored was very small, more people joined the church and stood
with me at the altar than there were members who were in attendance. The welcoming "amens" were weak on that Sunday, and for
the first time I got an understanding of the "we" "they" church syndrome. From that Sunday to approximately three years later, members were literally identified as being a "we" or a "they." All members were identified as either a "new member" or an "old member."
When I appointed committees, church members would attempt to
hold me to the task of balancing the committee with old members
and new members. This type of "we"/"they"and "us"/"them" literally existed until God, in time, dissolved it. It is an erroneous as-
sumption to think that all church members want the church to grow.
Those who have "been there" often do not want those who "come
there" to "be there." And when those who "come there" feel that
those who have "been there" do not want them to "be there," those
who "come there" "leave there." Oftentimes the comments are subtle.
At other times the comments that cause new members to feel uncom-
fortable are given in the name of the pastor. For example, someone
might say to a new member, "The pastor does not like it if we stand

up or start singing when the choir is singing their selection." This may be done by a supposed well-meaning member. Realistically, however, we must accept that some church members can be outright cruel, particularly when it come to protecting something they love and have taken ownership of, namely the church. The church must remain God's church. When we take ownership, then the emotions of jealousy and selfishness can surface. New members must be protected. The pastor must spend prime time protecting the new sheep that enter the front door lest they go out the back door.

A classic biblical example can be found in the book of Nehemiah. When they began to rebuild the temple, those who had (been there) not gone off into exile were the first to object.

> "But it came to pass, that when Sanballat heard that we builded the wall, he was wroth, and took great indignation, and mocked the Jews. And he spake before his brethren and the army of Samaria, and said, What do these feeble Jews? will they fortify themselves? will they sacrifice? will they make an end in a day? will they revive the stones out of the heaps of the rubbish which are burned? Now Tobiah the Ammonite was by him, and he said, Even that which they build, if a fox go up, he shall even break down their stone wall" (Neh 4:1-3).

Strategies for Assimilation

How then is assimilation best accomplished? To what does the pastor have to give personal attention and what can possibly be delegated? Gary McIntosh and Glen Martin in their book, *Finding Them and Keeping Them* list five noteworthy strategies for keeping them. Assimilation strategy one deals with helping people develop friendships. Assimilation strategy two deals with helping people become involved. Assimilation strategy three involves helping people belong. Assimilation strategy four involves helping people work together. Assimilation strategy five deals with helping people grow in their faith.[36] These strategies get right to the best point of attack. How do we process these strategies and what are some of the pitfalls?

Friendship. Friendship cannot be programmed or legislated. We can, however, learn from the behavioral sciences that people form friendships based on commonality and trust, such as being in the same geographical location, and having common needs and desires. The mere fact of being new members gives them something in common with other new members. They are all new members in a new church looking for friends and relationships and seeking to fill a spiritual void in their lives. However, the growth-oriented church cannot risk leaving friendships to be formed based on happenstance. Friendship formation should be intentional. One way of accomplishing this is to have a goal in the new member orientation class that each new member establish at least two friendships that the new member did not have before joining the church. The primary purpose of the new member orientation class should, therefore, be assimilation, not an introduction to doctrine. Most declining churches' new member classes focus on denominational polity and doctrine. At this point, however, assimilation is more critical.

Friends and the ability to make friends are closely akin to God's greatest commandment of love. Alan Loy McGinnis writes:

> People with no friends usually have a diminished capacity for sustaining any kind of love. They tend to go through a succession of marriages, be estranged from various family members, and have trouble getting along at work. On the other hand, those who learn how to love their friends tend to make long and fulfilling marriages, get along well with the people at work, and enjoy their children.[37]

God is love and love is God. Loving and caring are the heart of assimilation. The busy pastor cannot guarantee that love will be demonstrated by all of the members, but he can assure new members that as God's undershepherd, God loves them and he loves them. Because God is love, God blesses loving relationships. A biblical example is the love story of the book of Ruth.

Ruth was a Moabite girl who married an Israelite boy who had come to the land of Moab because of the famine in Bethlehem. Ruth's first husband died, but Ruth had established a loving bonded relationship with her mother-in-law, Naomi. When Naomi decided to return to Bethlehem, Ruth insisted on going with her. The scripture recalls her loving desire, "whither thou goest, I will go; and where thou lodgest, I will lodge: thy people shall be my people, and thy God my God:" (Ruth 1:16). Naomi and Ruth moved back to Bethlehem where Ruth met and married a rich Israelite and they lived happily together. Later they had a baby boy named Obed. Obed had a son named Jesse, who became the father of King David. Many, many years later, in Bethlehem, another baby was born named Jesus, a member of the family of Ruth and Boaz. Because of her love and her faithfulness, a Moabite girl, who was willing to leave home to live with her mother-in-law, brought the greatest love known, for Jesus is God, and God is Love, and Love is God. Likewise, because of the undershepherd's (pastor) and the leadership's faithfulness to indiscriminately protect, love, and care for all the new members, the church is perpetually blessed with additions to God's family.

Involving New Members in Role/Tasks. The second strategy for assimilation deals with involving new members in role tasks. Win Arn defines role/tasks as "a specific position, function, or responsibility in the church (choir, committee member, teacher, officer, etc.)."[38] In behavior pedagogy we learn to monitor student classroom behavior in a category called "on task" or "off task." The technique calls for the behavior-oriented teacher to define the behavior "on task" and then select a method of observation that would determine in a given classroom period the percentage of students who were on or off task. A certain percentage of students on task is used as a criteria for evaluating teacher effectiveness. Something similar needs to be established in the church to evaluate this area of assimilation. The basic premise for involving new members in task-oriented ministry is that the involvement edifies and satisfies the members. People want to feel useful. George Barna concurs by saying, "Unless you become involved in the activities of your church, you will never truly feel satisfied with your church."[39]

Foremost and beyond satisfying the needs of new members, workmanship is biblical. We are saved not by works; "Not of works, lest any man should boast. For we are his workmanship, created in Christ Jesus unto good works" (Eph 2:9-10). It is a "by," "through," and "unto" process. We are saved "by" grace. We are saved "through" faith, and we are saved "unto" good works. James said, "Faith without works is dead" (James 2:20). We are called to serve. Where do new members serve in the church where all the jobs are already taken? One of the many advantages of the growth-oriented Sunday School (G.O.S.S) vs the tradition-oriented Sunday School (T.O.S.S.) is that the G.O.S.S. is organized to create jobs. One worker is required for eight members enrolled. Every time a new class is formed approximately eight new meaningful role/tasks are created, such as teacher, co-teacher, secretary, outreach worker, inreach worker, prayer leader, and activities leader. One care group leader is needed for every five to ten enrollees. Starting new classes in a growth-oriented Sunday School is a highly effective method of accomplishing the assimilation process. This method simply cannot be ignored.

Helping People Become Involved. To help new members determine their roles, tasks, and places of service in the growth-oriented church, spiritual gifts seminar and classes should be offered as part of the assimilation process. C. Peter Wagner comments, "A spiritual gift is a special attribute given by the Holy Spirit to every member of the Body of Christ according to God's grace for use within the context of the Body."[40] Spiritual gifts seminars are a must in the assimilation process. Spiritual gifts study modules challenge new members to identify their gifts and motivate them to utilize their God-given talents. New members need to understand that God has given each believer at least one gift for the common good of the church. "But to each one is given the manifestation of Spirit for the common good" (1 Cor. 12:7). Pastors need to know that identifying and developing the spiritual gifts of the member are major components not only in assimilation but in the whole church growth processes.

In addition to sponsoring spiritual gifts seminars and workshops the pastor and church must have a spirit of openness to accept new ministries that arise out of the spiritual gifts discovered. Most traditional churches and insecure pastors are not open to new ministries which initiate from a new member.

The role/task strategy in the assimilation process is of utmost importance. Obviously immediate areas of roles and tasks such as the ushers, choir, recreation ministry, office volunteer, and mission groups should not be forgotten. A designated person should be held accountable for seeing that this particular part of the assimilation process happens. Designating a person creates yet another role.

Helping People Belong. Rather than add to established groups, new groups should be formed. Remember, social groups have boundaries. If possible, do not risk trying to add new members to established Sunday School classes. If the opportunity arises start a new Sunday School class. God said, "For where two or three are gathered together in my name, there am I in the midst of them" (Matt 18:20). Two or more present an opportunity to start a new Sunday School class, discipleship group, or general Bible study group. Small groups also address the first assimilation strategy of forming friendships. Small groups provide a support system for new members. Remember, new members need a support system because not everybody in the small group is happy that they have joined. More will be discussed about small groups in the next chapter.

Identification and Spiritual Growth. Assimilation strategy four, assimilation through identification, and strategy five, assimilation through spiritual growth, are both long-term strategies of assimilation. Both are necessary. Assimilation through identification strives to get the member to buy into the vision and direction of the church. More specifically, to become "sold out" on the church's purpose. Growing churches have a God-size vision and specific objectives for getting there. Growth-oriented churches have a mission statement, and everything they do should point back to that mission statement. Growth-oriented churches are known in the community in general as having a uniqueness or distinction such as having the largest Sunday School in the city or the best choirs in town. Whether the identification principle happens to be positive and spiritual, or negative and secular, part of the long- term assimilation process is for the member to "buy in" and be "sold out" on the church's identification labels. The prouder the members wear their church identification label, the longer they will remain a member of that particular church. Of course growth-oriented churches want all members to wear the church identification label of evangelism. Since growth-oriented churches have the ministry of intentional evangelism as their primary purpose, members must internalize ownership in this identification principle that simulates Jesus' mission.

Assimilation through spiritual growth is another long term strategy. In fact, discipleship is a part of the total assimilation process. Evangelism and assimilation must be balanced with discipleship. Spiritual growth through the formation of discipleship groups and solid biblical teachings are necessary for assimilation to be totally effective.

Stages of Assimilation

Assimilation can be viewed in three stages: the immediate stage, the transition stage, and the permanent (long term) stage. In the immediate stage, there are several immediate points of entry for new members: volunteer work in the office, responsibility for some short-term task for which there is recognition, singing in the choir, serving as an usher, and attending the new members orientation class. The transition stage includes joining a new Sunday School class, serving in a role/task assignment in that class, participating in a spiritual gifts seminar or workshop, and joining a discipleship group for spiritual growth. The permanent stage includes being an active part of the mission of the church, serving in a ministry leader capacity, matriculating through the discipleship training curriculum, and participating in the church's leadership programs, as well as continuing in selected activities from stages one and two.

Keys to Retention

Assimilation is about keeping new members once you get them. Hardaway offers the following relative to the issue of retention. "There are three keys to retaining members in the church: (1) keeping members involved in activities and relationships; (2) meeting the needs of members; and (3) avoiding making members mad. If a church does these three things well, it will not have to worry much about dropouts, because they will be few."[41]

Note, not much is being discussed about ministering to disgruntled (mad) and inactive members. This book is about being "faithful over a few things." That translates into putting first things first. If the few things are done faithfully, especially cherishing relationships, there will be only a small minority of people who fall into the disgruntled category. There are some good prototype modules that focus on this problem such as "the ingathering ministry" produced by the Southern Baptist Convention. Inactive members have a definite need that should be addressed by the church. More often than not, the pastor must wait until they come to themselves (Luke 15:17); pray for them, and welcome them if they return to the church.

Steps

Although it is impossible to put the assimilation processes into a rigid formula. William M. Eason offers a ten step plan that I think is noteworthy and maybe helpful.

Step One:	Picture taken, information form and orientation packet given on the Sunday new member joins
Step Two:	First Week
	a. "Opportunities for Service" brochure and new member pledge card mailed separately

b. Staff reviews new member names and pictures at staff meeting

Step Three: Second Week

a. Follow up on "Opportunities" brochure.

b. Information passed on to staff members who make the appropriate response or invitation

Step Four: Worship attendance tracked, with appropriate calls or visits made by Nurture and Care committee

Step Five: Follow-up stewardship calls every month to new members who have not sent in pledges

Step Six: Invitation to attend the orientation class

Step Seven: Invitation to new member party

Step Eight: Staff review of all new members in late summer for identification of potential leaders, who will then be invited to leadership party in the fall

Step Nine: Annual new member dinner in November

Step Ten: Invitation to newly formed classes or groups[42]

Research Data on Assimilation

The following research data taken from *An Executive Summary of Research into Why Do Some Churches Grow* conducted by the South Carolina Baptist Convention gives credence and support to the process of assimilation.

In Assimilation Efforts

We can safely say that 58% of those respondents are intentional about assimilating people into the church in that there is at least one person or committee responsible for keeping track of newcomers to make sure that they become a part of the church. The methods of choice: 55% said a new member class. Forty-one percent utilized the small group system. Thirty-six percent gave people a role or a task, 27% used a reception for new members, while 24% tried to develop a mentoring program.

Unfortunately, two-thirds of the churches (68%) said the pastor was the one responsible for this program. (We are challenged to think that a pastor can be effective in this and everything else under his charge.) Fully another 50% indicated that a Bible school class—or Bible study group— was responsible, while 38% said a deacon, shepherd, or elder was.

The growing churches (65% of them) and the largest churches (69% of them) were more likely to have made an intentional change recently in how they assimilate people. In contrast, the declining and smallest churches were less likely to have made any changes in their assimilation efforts. Only 38% of the SCBC churches made a change in assimilation. This compares to a majority of all the other churches, where 60% of them have made an intentional change in how they assimilate people.

Helping People Find a Place of Service
Helping people find a place of service has long been understood to be an important factor in helping churches to assimilate people and, ultimately, grow.
Forty-seven percent of the respondents indicate that they actively do this by holding a spiritual gifts seminar on occasion. Another 20% offer a spiritual gifts class on an ongoing basis.

These were active methods. More passive methods put the burden of finding a place of service on the person who wanted to serve. Forty-two percent said finding a place of service was available through counseling with the pastor. The fastest growing churches were more likely to offer the most active method—an ongoing spiritual gifts class. Slower growth, or declining churches, tended to not offer any ongoing counseling or class. Again, 64% said the senior pastor was responsible for the coordination and facilitation of a gift discovery process. (We can only imagine what could happen if pastors build teams to care for this and for assimilation.)

The larger churches were less likely to indicate that they relied on their pastors.

SCBC churches were less likely to have specific roles and tasks identified for people wanting to use their gifts when compared to the balance of those surveyed.

Larger churches were more likely to have identified written roles for ministry opportunities than small churches.[43]

Suggestions for Implementation and the Need to Monitor

Remember, one of the basic premises of this book is that pastors are the chief catalysts of growth in the church; therefore, pastors must manage their time to make sure that the absolute few things that cause church growth are done. With this in mind, the following is suggested:

A new member class that has assimilation as its main objective should be taught by the pastor and spouse if he or she is active in the ministry. The closest person that shares the pastor's growth vision for the church may co-teach with him, but the pastor must be the chief conductor of the new member orientation class. The new members class is simply the most advantageous position from which to orchestrate. It is not likely that anyone else will have the required sensitivity toward new members. In addition, the pastor can best articulate and sell the church's principles of identification and vision. From the position of teacher of the new members, the pastor can best orchestrate the involvement in small group and role/task assignments. Moreover, the pastor can provide the assurance of acceptability, love, and belonging.

The entire assimilation process must be thought of and treated like a ministry. Therefore, the assimilation ministry needs a director or coordinator. In growing churches, great budget consideration should be given to making this position a full-time paid staff person. This is just as important as a full-time minister of evangelism. In other words, the back door of the church is just as important as the front.

Monitoring assimilation is essential. Just as important as counting the number of new baptisms, we must also count our casualties. However, the emphasis on the maintenance process should not just be on the casualties. Monitoring our successes should help us continue to improve our assimilation process. Regarding this, there must be some accountability for the number of new members that attend new member orientation and the spiritual gifts seminar. There should be a count of the number of new members who are serving in a ministry or small group setting. The evaluation should include the new members who are participating in discipleship groups and have assimilated into the Sunday School.

One of the exit goals for the new member orientation class is to have met two to five new friends before the class can be completed. Monitoring must not just include numbers, but also faces and personalities. An effort must be made by the leadership, paid staff, deacons, and family ministry directors to know people by name and face. Video cameras can be helpful. Review photos and videos. Assimilation is important, and it must be intentional. Its effectiveness must be monitored and evaluated.

Again, the pastor cannot do everything, but he can do and assure that a few things are done well. He must assure that the process of assimilation is implemented and monitored.

In Summary

Assimilation in the church is that process that makes new members an accepted and valued part of the church as perceived, not by the church, but by new members themselves. If assimilation is not assured, evangelistic efforts become counterproductive. Assimilation is important because new members are the life-sustaining blood of the church. The process of assimilation has been discussed. Five strategies for assimilation were explored and three stages of assimilation were viewed. Retention was noted as a factor related to assimilation, and it was established that monitoring assimilation is absolutely essential.

Chapter 7

Create Small Groups

The Necessity of Small Groups for Effective Spiritual and Numerical Growth

Creating small groups is not an option for the church that desires spiritual and numerical growth. Some church growth consultants are of the opinion that small groups are not for every church. In my opinion, the question is not should we or should we not have small groups, rather, the more appropriate question might be to what extent will we be involved in a small group ministry. Some components of a small group ministry are inevitable in all churches. The choir and ushers are small groups. Among the few things that a church and her leadership must do for effective and maximum church growth is strengthen the area of small group ministries. Notice the terms "effective" and "maximum" church growth are emphasized. Earlier, the terms "spiritual" and "numerical" growth were stressed. Such descriptions are the result of small group ministries. Churches that do not desire maximum effective spiritual and numerical growth may not be inclined to actively focus and participate in small groups. Empirical research on small groups is very much in the embryonic stage. Research conducted by J. David Schmidt and Associates in 1965 on a population of 1,695 churches with a response rate of 26% (446 churches) reports the following in the area of support groups and small groups.

Slightly over a third (37%) of the churches did not have any small group ministry, while 63% did.

Most of the fastest growing churches (72%) have small group ministries. In contrast, fewer of the steady growth churches (51%) or declining churches (49%) have small group ministries. The median size of the churches <u>with</u> small groups was 235, while the median size of churches <u>without</u> small groups was 60.

Small groups is a relatively new phenomenon in most of the churches who responded. Sixty-five percent have had a small group ministry less than two years. Only 17% had such a ministry for <u>more than six years</u>. Has it had any impact on attendance? Forty-four percent said it had caused growth in their church, while 32% said it had little or no impact.

The fastest growing churches were more likely to say it caused growth—54% of them said this. Conversely, fewer of the declining churches (12%) or steady churches (36%) said it caused growth.[44]

The Reason for Creating Small Groups

Pastors and other church leaders who have a sincere desire to see their churches grow to the full potential will arrange and/or rearrange and redirect or further direct their time and energy to become faithful in creating small group ministries. This is based on the simple premise that the worship service itself, standing absolutely alone, cannot fulfill all of the biblical functions of the church.

Effective fellowship cannot be fulfilled in the worship service after attendance reaches a certain number. This number may vary depending on the pastor's skills and the structure of the worship. Regardless, there is a limit. There will be a plateau that a growing church will reach where the basic fellowship (the *koinonia*) begins to diminish. A word of caution about undermining fellowship. Often we do not elevate fellowship to its level of importance because we think of it as embracing, handshaking, greeting each other with holy kisses and the like. We think we can accomplish this with an excited five minute intrusion into the worship service. We can do this and still remain strangers in the pews. What a tragedy, brothers and sisters in Christ and strangers in the pews. Casual or planned greeting of each other in Jesus' name does not fit the meaning of *koinonia* in the New Testament. *Koinonia* means sharing and caring in a demonstrative way. It is derived from *koinonos* which means partner, companion, partaker, sharer, road buddy. The best planned worship service cannot fulfill the real need of fellowship.

Worship, also, is not and cannot produce effective discipleship. Disciples, not church members, is what God has called us to become. The best pulpit teaching ministry will fall short in fulfilling the command of The Great Commission if it is not supported and/or supplemented with some small group interaction.

Functions of Small Group Ministries

Assimilation, discussed in the previous chapter, is impossible to accomplish without small groups. Support, protection and encouragement for new members and seasoned members can best take place in small groups. The five essential functions of the church are evangelism, discipleship, ministry, fellowship, and worship. Four out of five can best be accomplished in small groups rather than the worship assembly. Only worship can best take place in the total gathering of the assembly. Worth noting is that small groups should not try to become small worship ministries. Worship is not the task of small groups.

What is a small group? Small groups are not discipleship groups, although a discipleship group may be a small group. Small groups are not Sunday School classes, although a Sunday School class may be a small group. Sounds confusing? Not really. The definition is tied to the goal. The goal of a small group is to become biblical in an interpersonal relationship (i.e. loving one another, which will express itself in bearing one another's burden, edifying one another, praying for one another, rejoicing with one another, comforting one another, etc.). As a rule, Sunday School classes and discipleship groups are limited in focus and time relative to fulfilling the essential goal of small group ministries.

Definition and Analysis of Small Group Ministries

The Church Growth Institute in its practical manual *How to Start or Evaluate a Small Group Ministry* offers the following definition and analysis:

> A small group is a face-to-face gathering of 3 to 12 people on a regular time schedule where a sense of accountability to each other and Jesus Christ is present.

The key elements of this definition are:

- **Face-to face:** people interface with each other directly and personally.
- **3-12 people:** the group is small enough for face-to-face relationships to take place.
- **Regular time schedule:** the group meets a minimum of two times per month.
- **Sense of accountability:** the group has a feeling of concern and responsibility to each other.[45]

The Explosive Church to the Third Power

As previously indicated, small groups are inevitable in church life. There are small groups and there are smaller groups. There are small groups that are task oriented, and there is the possibility and need to create smaller groups for the primary function of fulfilling the New Testament meaning of *koinonia*. C. Peter Wagner offers the following formula that gives clarification to the concept of small groups. The formula is "Celebration + Congregation + Cell = Church."[46] I have developed my own slant on this formula and that is Celebration x Congregation x Cell = C^3, creating an Explosive Church.

The celebration component represents the all important worship gathering. As stated earlier in this book, worship is God's party. The Bible admonishes us in Hebrews 10:25, "Not forsaking the assembling of ourselves together,". Worship remains the greatest entry point for church membership. Celebratory or joyous worship is a powerful component of church growth. Small groups are not designed for worship. They are designed for basically all other functions except worship. This does not mean that small groups should not pray and give testimonies and praises to God. Celebration, however; is best fulfilled when all the small groups come together as one to worship God. This is traditionally the eleven o'clock Sunday morning worship setting. But what happens between the Sundays? This is when the congregation that is described in the Celebration x Congregation x Cell = Explosive Church formula becomes a distinguishable activity.

This second "C" in the church to the third power (CxCxC=C^3) formula is most often represented by task-oriented small groups that have been established to carry out certain specific maintenance functions. These combined groups are referred to as the congregation. Congregation is a technical term for the internal structure of the church, to which approximately 40 to 120 members belong. Every member of the church should belong to one of the *congregations* within the church."[47] Such groups include the worship supporting cast (choir and ushers), governing boards and advisory councils (deacons, trustees, stewards, elders, etc.), committees, and other established ministries. The most accessible is the Sunday School. These groups, although task oriented, play another significant role in the life of the church. They are generally small enough (ranging from 15 to 100 people) to lose their anonymity and gain a sense of personal fellowship.

"In the congregation the anonymity is lost. If believers miss two or three celebrations in a row, no one is the wiser. But if they miss two or three meetings of the 'congregation,' they are worried over, called upon, prayed for, and made to understand that there are people around who care. Deep down, everyone needs to have others know his or her name and use it. The congregation is the place where people know each other's names.[48]"

Notice, growth can and should take place both at the level of celebration and the congregational fellowship level. These levels should combine their efforts and work on one accord to produce maximum growth potential. The choir should work heart-to-heart and hand-in-hand with the worship to enhance the celebration. Therefore, plan to grow the music department, but do not just depend on people who are interested and skilled to join the choir. Plan growth at every level and in every auxiliary. Real growth is not incidental. Plan to grow, and plan to grow congregational small groups. Once again, the Sunday School in most churches is probably the most accessible established small group that can be and should be organized for growth. We have already given much discussion to Tradition-Oriented Sunday School (T.O.S.S.) vs. Growth-Oriented Sunday School (G.O.S.S.). The church and her leadership should never neglect the Sunday School small group setting as a fantastic growth arena.

A word of caution relative to the congregation level of small groups: oftentimes these small groups suffer from what may be called the Catch 22 syndrome. The problem is the same thing that makes the fellowship good also prevents acceptability of new members. This is a basic sociological phenomena. Small groups wherein members find identity and a sense of belonging become protective of that which they value. The elements that hold them in the fellowship prevent others from entering the fellowship. Experience teaches that well-meaning choir leaders, Sunday School class teachers, usher chairpersons, etc., simply do not follow-up and call new members who repeatedly sign up to join their task-oriented group. Even when attending established Sunday School classes, new members report simply not feeling welcome. It is hard for some to crack through the semipermeable barrier established by small groups. Whether the church decides to attempt to assimilate new members into existing groups or prefers to channel them into new groups, all small groups should be taught and trained to accept new members wholeheartedly.

The third "C" in our church to the third power formula represents the cell. Cell groups are even smaller than the middle "C" congregational groups. Cell groups should under no circumstance have more than twelve members, otherwise the main purpose is defeated by the numbers. Cell groups may be conducted in a variety of ways, but the main agenda is relationship building. The key word is love. The purpose is to fulfill the often overlooked or underemphasized portion of The Great Commission, "teach them to observe all things" (Matt. 28:20). The specific objective is the fulfillment of that portion of the greatest commandment to "love one another, as I have loved you," (John 13:34). Larry R. Chards, a leading advocate of small groups, defines the cell as "eight to twelve believers gathered to minister to each other to grow in their sensed love and unity, and to encourage one another to full commitment to Christ."[49]

The small cell group ministry has yet to reach a status of acceptability in most traditional churches. In most churches, the creation of a small group cell ministry means initiating radical change. To accomplish this, leadership must become risk takers. Establishing a cell group ministry tends to separate the shakers and movers from the more passive church growth leaders. Effective small cell group ministry probably represents the most untapped potential for church growth among traditional mainline churches. Many small cell group ministries exist and there are some excellent existing church models. For example, from data reported as far back as 1984, "The Full Gospel Central Church in Seoul, Korea is considered the largest single church in the world, numbering seventy-five thousand members, with 17 pastors, 45 elders, and 3,400 deacons. These numbers would seem to be far too unwieldy for effective handling, but pastoring or shepherding them has proved possible because of their cell subdivisions."[50]

Currently, in America, Bill Hybel and the Willow Creek Community Church in Illinois is representative among today's leaders in the small cell group ministry. According to Elmer L. Towns, writing about today's ten most innovative churches, Willow Creek, "the second largest church in America has a weekly attendance of over 14,000.

Willow Creek Community Church is also one of the most innovative churches in America because of its creative programming."[51] Towns, however, listed the most effective cell ministry in America as the Hope Community Church in Portland, Oregon, pastored by Dale Galloway.

> Galloway was asked to describe how cell ministries worked in his church. He responded: "Cells are not another ministry of the church, cells are the church." At present they have almost 485 cells with 4,800 persons in weekly attendance in cell meetings. Galloway's vision, when he began the church in the early 70's, was to have one cell group for every ten members; and today that ratio still holds true. They are called Tender Loving Care (TLC) groups. Both members and visitors attend whatever TLC group they desire. This strategy is in contrast to Willow Creek Community Church in South Barrington, IL, where the church directs people to certain groups.[52]

The structural concept of the cell group is not new to the traditional church. What is new is its potential for growth. Historically, churches have had small cell groups with a variety of names for an equal variety of reasons. Team and team captains have been used for the purpose of collecting dues or for collecting money for fund raising campaigns. Birthday clubs, zone ministries, kinship circles, and sheparding nurturing groups are but a few. Among Southern Baptist Convention churches that represent the largest Protestant group in the world, the Deacon Family Ministry Plan is widely used in an effort to fulfill this purpose. The major pitfalls in most of these plans is the failure to (1) have enough trained leaders, (2) remain small, and (3) stay focused on the purpose. For example, the Greenforest Baptist Church in Decatur, GA that has grown from a handful of members (25) to an active membership of 4,000 in the last 16 years adopted the Deacon Family Ministry Plan from its humble beginning. In calculating, 4,000 members divided by 16 years, equals a growth rate of about 250 new members per year. Acknowledging the need for one deacon for each 10 new members, the church would need to produce 25 new deacons per year (250 new members divided by 10 deacons = 25 deacons). At the rate of 25 deacons per year times 16 years, the church, if it were effectively abiding by the numbers required, would have 400 deacons. The church currently has approximately 50 active deacons. While the Deacon Family Ministry Plan is considered to be the stabilizing force of the church, the individual ministries are simply too large to function as cell groups. The church is currently seeking new deacons as well as expanding the level of leadership to produce yokepersons who would serve as leader of a yoke circle. The yoke circle would be a subdivision under the deacon family ministry and absolutely have no more than 10 persons per circle. The yoke circle will meet at least once a month, most likely in a home, for two hours with the primary goal being relationship building and learning to love one another. Leaders (deacons and yokeperson) will be trained first in discipleship and in relationship building skills. A brief training format on how to build relationship skills is included later in this chapter.

A Justification (Need) for Home Cell Groups

Although some may be critical and fearful of the small group home cell approach, it is without question biblically and theologically sound. From a church perspective, it is authentic, and when we view the body of Christ holistically, we cannot deny the need.

<u>A Biological Biblical Motif.</u>   Let's begin by looking at the small group home cell from a biological perspective with a biblical motif. All living things are made up of cells. The church is an organism, not an organization. All organisms grow by cell division. Cells are composed of the genetic blueprint (DNA) that determine the basic character of the larger body. The blueprint for the church is love. The genetic blueprint is housed in the cell's nucleus. The nucleus of the church is relationships. Cells have a membrane that protects and determines what should enter and what should not enter. Christians need protection from the wiles of Satan, "For we wrestle not against flesh and blood, but against principalities, against powers, against the rulers of the darkness of this world, against spiritual wickedness in high places" (Eph 6:12). The kingdom of God only permits those to enter who have formed a personal relationship with Jesus. Another characteristic of cells is that they multiply themselves. Christians should multiply themselves, and the local church should multiply herself, "Ye shall be witnesses" (Acts 1:8). The cell must work in harmony with the tissues, organs, and other systems of the body, for the whole to operate efficiently. Likewise, the church according to Ephesians 4:16, "from whom the whole body, being fitted and held together by that which every joint supplies, according to the proper

working of each individual part, causes the growth of the body for the building up of itself in love." (NAS). God inspired the writer, the apostle Paul, to use the biological body as his major theological motif illustrating the church. Paul writes in 1 Corinthians:

> "For as the body is one, and hath many members, and all the members of that one body, being many, are one body: so also is Christ. For by one Spirit are we all baptized into one body, whether we be Jews or Gentiles, whether we be bond or free; and have been all made to drink into one Spirit. For the body is not one member, but many. If the foot shall say, Because I am not the hand, I am not of the body; is it therefore not of the body? And if the ear shall say, Because I am not the eye, I am not of the body; is it therefore not of the body? If the whole body were an eye, where were the hearing? If the whole were hearing, where were the smelling? But now hath God set the members every one of them in the body, as it hath pleased him. And if they were all one member, where were the body? But now are they many members, yet but one body. And the eye cannot say unto the hand, I have no need of thee: nor again the head to the feet, I have no need of you. Nay, much more those members of the body, which seem to be more feeble, are necessary: And those members of the body, which we think to be less honourable, upon these we bestow more abundant honour; and our uncomely parts have more abundant comeliness. For our comely parts have no need: but God hath tempered the body together, having given more abundant honour to that part which lacked: That there should be no schism in the body; but that the members should have the same care one for another. And whether one member suffer, all the members suffer with it; or one member be honoured, all the members rejoice with it. Now ye are the body of Christ, and members in particular" (1 Cor 12:12-27).

God, through the apostle Paul, teaches us about the function and operation of the church using the human body parts as an analogy. He wants us to know that we have particular parts, and all are dependent upon one another. We are not only interrelated, we are dependent on one another. When the choir suffers, the worship service suffers; when the deacons suffer, the ministries suffer, and the whole body is affected. When one small group in the church is affected, the whole body is affected. Moreover, when one individual is affected, the whole should be affected. When one individual rejoices the whole body should rejoice. This does not happen in large groups due to a lack of communication and lack of sensitivity. Thus small groups and even smaller groups within the body are essential. For example, learning to rejoice when good things happen to others is a difficult Christian behavior to learn. When bad things happen to others and we know about it, usually there is some degree of sympathy if not empathy. But we do not easily rejoice when good things happen to others. We need small and smaller groups to learn and practice this behavior.

A Biblical Pattern (Jethro the Midianite). Biblically speaking, Jethro the Midianite, set the pattern for small group administration in the Book of Exodus when he instructed Moses on the principle of delegation.18:17-26:

> "And Moses' father in law said unto him, The thing that thou doest is not good. Thou wilt surely wear away, both thou, and this people that is with thee: for this thing is too heavy for thee; thou art not able to perform it thyself alone. Hearken now unto my voice, I will give thee counsel, and God shall be with thee: Be thou for the people to God-ward, that thou mayest bring the causes unto God: And thou shalt teach them ordinances and laws, and shalt shew them the way wherein they must walk, and the work that they must do. Moreover thou shalt provide out of all the people able men, such as fear God, men of truth, hating covetousness; and place such over them, to be rulers of thousands, and rulers of hundreds, rulers of fifties, and rulers of tens: And let them judge the people at all seasons: and it shall be, that every great matter they shall bring unto thee, but every small matter they shall judge: so shall it be easier for thyself, and they shall bear the burden with thee. If thou shalt do this thing, and God command thee so, then thou shalt be able to endure, and all this people shall also go to their place in peace. So Moses hearkened to the voice of his father in law, and did all that he had said. And Moses chose able men out of all Israel, and made them heads over the

people, rulers of thousands, rulers of hundreds, rulers of fifties, and rulers of tens. And they judged the people at all seasons: the hard causes they brought unto Moses, but every small matter they judged themselves" (Exo 18:17-26).

Small cell group administration is what I call ultimate delegation. Small cell groups must have a degree of self-governance to be ultimately effective, yet they must always be accountable to the body and the pastor.

<u>Psychological and Sociological Behavior.</u>   It has been said that no man is an island, no man stands alone. Biblically, God responded to this psychological phenomenon when He made and gave man a helpmate (woman) and the privilege of procreation. We need each other. Societal trends such as the changing family structure, mobile lifestyles, devaluing of morals, no standard for behavior, and a spectator-oriented culture all justify the need for cell groups that practice loving one another.

> "Two are better than one; because they have a good reward for their labour. For if they fall, the one will lift up his fellow: but woe to him that is alone when he falleth; for he hath not another to help him up. Again, if two lie together, then they have heat: but how can one be warm alone? And if one prevail against him, two shall withstand him; and a threefold cord is not quickly broken" (Eccl 4:9-12)

There is no question about it, we need one another and we need to love one another. How many times does God have to tell us something before we believe it? How many times does the all-powerful God have to show us something in His holy word before we do it? Prayerfully only one time. Repeatedly, God tells us to be concerned about one another. The following scriptures are a few direct "one another" admonishments:

1 Corinthians 12:25 That there should be no schism in the body; but that the members should have the same care <u>one for another.</u>

1 Corinthians 16:20 All the brethren greet you. Greet ye <u>one another</u> with an holy kiss.

Galatians 5:13 For, brethren, ye have been called unto liberty; only use not liberty for an occasion to the flesh, but by love serve <u>one another</u>.

Galatians 5:15 But if ye bit and devour <u>one another</u>, take heed that ye be not consumed one of another.

Ephesians 5:21 Submitting yourselves <u>one to another</u> in the fear of God.

1 Thessalonians 4:18 Wherefore comfort <u>one another</u> with these words.

1 Thessalonians 5:11 Wherefore comfort yourselves together, and edify <u>one another</u>, even as also ye do.

1 Thessalonians 5:13 And to esteem them very highly in love for their work's sake, And be at peace <u>among yourselves</u>.

Hebrews 10:24 And let us consider <u>one another</u> to provoke unto love and to good works:

James 5:9 Grudge not <u>one against another</u>, brethren, lest ye be condemned: behold, the judge standeth before the door.

James 5:16 Confess your faults one to another, and pray <u>one for another</u>, that ye may be healed. The effectual fervent prayer of a righteous man availeth much.

1 Peter 4:9 Use hospitality <u>one to another</u> without grudging.

Romans 12:10 Be kindly affectioned <u>one to another</u> with brotherly love; in honour preferring one another;

Romans 14:13 Let us not therefore judge <u>one another</u> any more: but judge this rather, that no man put a stumblingblock or an occasion to fall in his brother's way.

Romans 14:19 Let us therefore follow after the things which make for peace, and things wherewith <u>one may edify another</u>.

Romans 15:14 And I myself also am persuaded of you, my brethren, that ye also are full of goodness, filled with all knowledge, able also to admonish <u>one another</u>.

<u>The Early Church's Pattern.</u>   The early church had no problem "having church" in small cell-like home groups. The church was never

intended to be brick and mortar. Nowhere in the New Testament is the church thought of as a building. The church is described as a body and a bride, but never a building. The Greek New Testament has only one word translated church—the word is *ekklesia* which means "called out." "An analysis of all the 112 occurrences of *ekklesia* translated *church* in the New Testament show that they may be divided into three categories: (1) The Church of Jesus Christ universal, (2) The Church identified with a city or town, and (3) The Church in the home."[53]

A quick glance at a few scriptures from the New Testament church history book, the Book of Acts, offers us some illumination on small groups in the early church. Notice the references to small groups as well as to meeting in houses or homes.

> **Acts 2:46a** And they, continuing daily with one accord in the temple, and breaking bread from house to house,

> **Acts 3:1** Now Peter and John went up together into the temple at the hour of prayer, being the ninth hour.

> **Acts 4:34-35** Neither was there any among them that lacked: for as many as were possessors of lands or houses sold them, and brought the prices of the things that were sold, And laid them down at the apostles' feet: and distribution was made unto every man according as he had need.

> **Acts 5:11** And great fear came upon all the church, and upon as many as heard these things.

> **Acts 5:21** And when they heard that, they entered into the temple early in the morning, and taught. But the high priest came, and they that were with him, and called the council together,

> **Acts 5:41-42** And they departed from the presence of the council, rejoicing that they were counted worthy to suffer shame for his name. And daily in the temple, and in every house, they ceased not to teach and preach Jesus Christ.

> **Acts 9:10,11a,b** And there was a certain disciple at Damascus, named Ananias; and to him said the Lord in a vision, Ananias. And he said, Behold, I am here, Lord. And the Lord said unto him, Arise, and go into the street which is called Straight, and inquire in the house...

Acts 9:17 And Ananias went his way, and entered into the house; and putting his hands on him said, Brother Saul, the Lord, even Jesus, that appeared unto thee in the way as thou camest, hath sent me, that thou mightest receive thy sight, and be filled with the Holy Ghost.

Acts 10:23 Then called he them in, and lodged them. And on the morrow Peter went away with them, and certain brethren from Joppa accompanied him.

Acts 13:2 As they ministered to the Lord, and fasted, the Holy Ghost said, Separate me Barnabas and Saul for the work whereunto I have called them.

Ron Trudinger in his marvelous little book entitled *Cells For Life* reports numbers of cases of ministry that took place in the home. He writes:

In the last chapter of his letter to the Romans Paul writes: "Greet Priscilla and Aquila...also greet the church that is in their house..." Elsewhere he mentions the church in Nympha's or Nymphas', as some mess. Read) house; and, when writing to Philemon, "the church in your house."
Most of us remember with sympathy Eutychus' dropping off to sleep during Paul's long preaching and falling from the window sill of the third floor room where the local church was meeting. This seems to have been a private home.

Turning to the Gospels, we find that although Jesus Himself taught and preached in synagogues, the temple and in the open air, He favoured private houses for much of His ministry. Such home occasions resulted, in the case of Zacchaeus, in the winning of the whole household to God. Also He frequently used homes for teaching and explanation, i.e. in Matt. 13:16: "He left the multitudes and went into the house, and His disciples came...saying 'explain to us the parable of the tares of the field....'"

Jesus' healing also was often in homes, as in the instance when four men let down the paralytic through the roof.[54]

<u>The Jesus Model (Twelve Chosen and Trained)</u>. The supreme model for small cell group ministry is the Jesus model. As disciples of Christ, the very essence of our existence is to model Christ. We are easily reminded that even though Jesus spoke at times to crowds, He chose only twelve apostles. Twelve were chosen to be trained in the intimate circle of the master. Jesus also had an inner circle within the inner circle. When Jesus got ready to be shown in all His glory, to give the world a foretaste of glory divine, He chose only three, Peter, James, and John, to go upon the Mount of Transfiguration (Mark 9:2). In the Garden of Gethsemane He went only so far with the entire group, then He took the inner cell group a little further. If we are to go a little further in church growth we must go a little further than celebration (worship) and congregation (task-oriented small group). We must venture into the most conducive ministry for loving one another and building relationships, namely smaller cell group ministries.

How to Get Started Creating a Small Group Ministry

The final section of this chapter addresses the question of *how*. How do I get started? Where do I begin? First I would suggest you make a commitment to small group ministry. Second, realize that any changes that are to be made must be made gently, in love, with the full sensitivity to the dynamics of change discussed in the third chapter and elsewhere in this book. The church must be prepared for any changes that are to take place. Prepare the church and lay leaders through intentional teaching, with no deception or manipulation, of the value of developing and creating small group fellowships. Pray for guidance and the power of the Holy Spirit to lead and guide you. Trudinger writes, "The first step, clearly, is to *teach* the concepts of discipleship, maturing, relationships, spiritual authority and the need for pastoral care to be given to every individual church member. You cannot just intellectually argue people into accepting these Kingdom principles. The Holy Spirit whom Jesus called the Spirit of truth will have to open their hearts and instruct them."[55]

After you have begun the processes of preparation, evaluate the effectiveness of the existing small groups in the church. As mentioned earlier, all churches have small groups, such as choir groups, usher groups, or discipleship groups. The concept is to begin with what already exists. Most existing small groups are task-related groups. A good point of initiation would be to teach task related groups to also become caring fellowship groups. Choirs and ushers could be subdivided according to sections or Sundays on duty to help accomplish this purpose. Existing Sunday School classes should be downsized to facilitate fellowship and nurturing. Teach task-related groups to monitor the general participation of their members. If an existing task related group member drops out of service, that is a sign that something may be awry in their life, and an opportunity for ministry is present. A change in service and participation patterns of any group member is an open door for practicing loving one another. All existing groups that are smaller than the worship celebration service should develop *koinonia* components.

Continuing with the concept of building on what exists, review the organizational structure to see what groups currently exist for the purpose of fellowship. Such groups may include birthday clubs, concern circle groups, zone circles, kinship circles, deacon family ministries, shepherding ministries, yokepersons ministries, etc. The key is to evaluate their effectiveness. Do they meet the criteria for small group ministries that we have set forth and discussed in this chapter?

Evaluating Small Group Ministries

The Church Growth Institute offers the following guidelines and format in evaluating your small group ministry that may be helpful.

1. Total number of small groups. As a rule of thumb, a church needs seven small groups for every 100 adults present at its Sunday morning worship services. This is often stated as a ratio of 7:100. For example, a church averaging 150 adults at Sunday morning worship services needs 10 small groups. (150 divided by 100 = 1.5x7 = 10.5).

2. New Small Groups. A church may find that it has enough small groups based on the 7:100 ratio noted above. However, this is not the total picture. Since older small groups tend to resist the inclusion of newer people, it is important to have newer groups available that are open to the addition of new people.

As a general rule of thumb, a small group will close to the addition of new people between the eighteenth and twenty-fourth month of its existence. Thus, a church could have enough small groups, but if they are all over one and a half years old, the church would still have a problem.

In general, 40% of a church's small groups should be less than two years old. This is expressed by the ratio of 2:5. Two out of every five groups should be less than two years old.

3. <u>Total number of participants</u>. Even with the best small group ministry available, not all of your adults will choose to participate. Generally, a healthy church will have 50% of its adult worshipers participating in its small group ministry. This is often expressed by the ratio of 1:2.[56]

Review and evaluation will reveal the weaknesses in your small group fellowship ministries. This is where your work begins. After the initial groundwork has been done, your next step is to identify and train leaders. Leadership makes the difference. Small groups will not operate effectively without effective leaders. Leaders must first be disciples. They must be learners and followers of Christ and willing to teach others to become the same. All leaders must complete at least one discipleship training course. This is a must. Just as the pastor is the catalyst to church growth, so are the small group leaders to fellowship groups. It is recommended that the pastor lead a group modeling the process he would like to see carried out in each small group. Remember, small groups are created for the purpose of fellowship. When small groups meet, regardless of what other agenda may be presented, over fifty percent of the time must be spent building relationships. The key to building relationships is sharing. Leaders must be trained in building relationship skills. The Church Growth Institute offers a step-by-step format for building relationships.[57]

Steps for Implementation

To summarize what has been said concerning how to get started, let me offer the following step-by-step process:

Step One   Seek God's direction and help.

Step Two   Develop a vision and mission statement.

Step Three	Educate the church and her leaders (Share the Vision).
Step Four	Review and evaluate existing small groups.
Step Five	Develop a *koinonia* component for existing task related small groups.
Step Six	Redirect the focus of existing small fellowship groups that may be unfocused or off track.
Step Seven	Develop specific structural, administrative, and operational guidelines for new fellowship groups.
Step Eight	Identify and select potential leaders.
Step Nine	Train potential leaders.
Step Ten	Teach a small group and model the expected process
Step Eleven	Identify a potential director of small group ministries. (Write a job description for this position).
Step Twelve	Delegate as much of the responsibility as possible without losing effectiveness.
Step Thirteen	Implement a plan to continually start new groups.
Step Fourteen	Develop and implement a plan of ongoing program (small group ministry) evaluation.

Critics have said that small groups are not for everybody. True, if the church has 100 to 200 members and does not plan to grow, there is no need to intentionally create small fellowship groups. Others have criticized small groups based on the risk of the development of cliques. The possibility of selfish pockets of members does exist. However, the most prominent reason why most churches do not create small fellowship groups is insecurity on the part of the pastor and leaders. Once again, leadership makes the difference. If the pastor and leaders are God-directed and Holy Ghost filled, they will have a spiritual internalization that God wants His church to grow. A principle of church growth says that to get larger you have to get smaller. This means that as a church gets larger, it must, in turn, develop small groups. This is why the pastor and the leaders must be faithful over this one of a few things, for He has indeed promised that if we will be "faithful over a few things, I will make thee ruler over many things: enter thou into the joy of thy lord" (Matt 25:21).

In Summary

Creating small groups is not an option for the church that desires spiritual and numerical growth. Some components of a small group ministry are inevitable in all churches. Among the few things that a church and her leadership must do for effective and maximum church growth is to give major attention to the principles of creating small group ministries. A small group is a face-to-face gathering of three to twelve people on a regular time schedule wherein a sense of accountability for each other and Jesus Christ is present. The reasons for small groups have been stated, and the task of small groups was described. The scope of the small group ministry was explained in terms of the "church to the third power" (Celebration x Congregation x Cells = Church[3]). A justification for home cell groups was explored based on psychological and sociological needs and biblical early church patterns, and how to start small groups and evaluate them was discussed. A step-by-step process of implementation was also offered.

Epilogue

No Principle is an Island

God's promise is if we are faithful with a few things, He will put us in charge of many things and we will share in His happiness (Matthew 25:21). What are the few things?

1. Cherish and Prioritize Relationships
2. Establish a Knowledge-Based Teach/Preaching Foundation
3. Initiate Change
4. Prioritize Expressive Praise and Pray in Faith
5. Orchestrate Intentional Evangelism and Outreach Ministries
6. Assure and Monitor Assimilation
7. Create Small Groups

No principle is an island. While each principle is unique, they are interrelated and interdependent. For example, in most churches expressive praise will not become a priority unless people are taught to praise God and change is initiated. Orchestrated evangelism and outreach are totally dependent on the power of the Holy Spirit. Without expressive praise and praying in faith, believers will not have access to this power. If the church fails to faithfully orchestrate intentional evangelism, there will be no one to faithfully assimilate. Assimilation is, then, dependent on evangelism. If relationships are not cherished by the leaders, little if any nurturing will take place in small group fellowships. Finally, we must realize that salvation is our ultimate goal, and the preaching of the gospel is the power unto salvation.

Each task must be faithfully implemented for the church to grow. There are no short cuts. The chain is only as strong as its weakest link. Be faithful over all of the few things.

Endnotes

1. Jack *Smith, Friends* Forever: Studies in Relational Evangelism (Atlanta: Evangelism Section, Home Mission Board, Southern Baptist Convention, 1994), 15.
2. Ibid., 16-18.
3. Elmer L. *Towns, An Inside Look at Ten of Today's Most Innovative* Churches (Ventura, CA, Regal Books, 1990), 228.
4. Ibid., 232.
5. Ken Hemphill, *The Antioch Effect: 8 Characteristics of Highly Effective* Churches, (Nashville: Broadman & Holman Publishers, 1994), 110.
6. Ibid., 112.
7. Gary McIntoch and Glen *Martin, Finding Them, Keeping Them: Effective Strategies for Evangelism and Assimilation in the Loc*al Church (Nashville: Broadman & Holman Publishers, 1992), 6.
8. Sadie *McCalep, How to Grow a Sunday School in Your Church: Neighborhood* Outreach (Nashville: 1992), 7.
9. Carlyle Fielding Stew*art III, African American Church Growth: 12 Principles for Prophetic* Ministry (Nashville: Abingdon Press, 1994), 22.
10. Words, Samuel J. Stone. Tune, Samuel S. Wesley, "The Church's One Foundation."
11. Words, Edward Mote. Tune, William B. Bradbury, "The Solid Rock."
12. Dr. Jonathan Jackson, Interdenominational Theological Center, Lectures, 1979.
13. Gen*e Mims, Kingdom Principles for Chur*ch Growth (Nashville: Convention Press, 1994), 6.
14. "Sunday School Plan Book," The Sunday School Board, Southern Baptist Convention (Nashville: Convention Press, Annual).
15. John Sullivan, "Church Growth Conference," Ft. Mill, SC, Home Mission Board, Southern Baptist Convention, September 5, 1995.
16. Schaller, Lyle, The Parish Paper, 1995
17. John Sullivan, "Church Growth Conference," Ft. Mill, SC., Home Mission Board, Southern Baptist Convention, September 5, 1995.
18. Jack Taylor, *The Hallelujah Factor* (Nashville: Broadman Press, 1983), 16-17.
19. Ibid., 42.
20. Ibid., 13.
21. Ibid., 92.
22. Ibid., 13.
23. Avery T. Willis, Jr., *MasterLife I*, (Nashville: Discipleship and Family Development Division, The Sunday School Board of the Southern Baptist Convention, 1982), 168.
24. Ibid., 168.
25. Ken Hemphill, *The Antioch Effect: 8 Characteristics of Highly Effective Churches* (Nashville: Broadman & Holman Publishers, 1994), 72.
26. Sadie McCalep, *How to Grow a Sunday School in Your Church: Neighborhood Outreach* (Nashville: 1992), 11.
27. Darrell W. Robinson, *People Sharing Jesus* (Nashville: Thomas Nelson Publishers, 1995). 21
28. H. Gerald Colbert, Editorial in *Michigan Baptist Advocate* (June 1993).

29. Sadie McCalep, *How to Grow a Sunday School in Your Church: Neighborhood Outreach* (Nashville: 1992), 11.
30. Ibid., 12
31. Ben Wilkinson, *Personal Evangelism*, American Society of Biblical Studies (Decatur, GA: PEF Publications Ministry, 1983), 46.
32. Sadie McCalep, *How to Grow a Sunday School in Your Church: Neighborhood Outreach* (Nashville: 1992), 14-15, 17.
33. *Continuing Witness Training*, Ron Johnson, Editor. Home Mission Board of the Southern Baptist Convention, 1982.
34. Darrell W. Robinson, *People Sharing Jesus* (Nashville: Thomas Nelson Publishers, 1995).
35. Hardaway, *Church Growth Principles: Separating Fact From Fiction* (Nashville: Broadman Press, 1991), 138.
36. Gary McIntosh and Glen Martin, *Finding Them, Keeping Them: Effective Strategies for Evangelism and Assimilation in the Local Church* (Nashville: Broadman & Holman Publishers, 1992), 16-17.
37. Alan Loy McGinnis, *The Friendship Factor* (Minneapolis: Augsburgh Publishing House), 9.
38. Win Arn, *The Church Growth Ratio Book* (Pasadena: Church Growth, Inc., 1987), 10.
39. George Barna, *How to Find Your Church* (Minneapolis: Worldwide Publications, 1989), 93.
40. C. Peter Wagner, *Your Spiritual Gifts Can Help Your Church Grow* (Ventura, CA: Regal Books, 1979), 42.
41. C. Kirk Hardaway, *Church Growth Principles: Separating Fact from Fiction* (Nashville: Broadman Press, 1991), 143.
42. William M. Eason, *The Church Growth Handbook*,(Abingdon Press, Nashville, 1990), 36-37.
43. J. David Schmidt and Associates, South Carolina Baptist Convention, "An Executive Summary of Research into Why Do Some Churches Grow".
44. Ibid.
45. Rodney J. Dean and Gary L. McIntosh, *How to Start or Evaluate a Small Group Ministry* (Lynchburg, VA: Church Growth Institute, 1991), 27.
46. C. Peter Wagner, *Your Church Can Grow* (Ventura, CA: Gospel Light Publishers, 1976), 111.
47. Kent R. Hunter, *Foundations for Church Growth: Biblical Basics for the Local Church*, (Corunna, IN: Church Growth Center), 194.
48. Ibid., 116.
49. Ibid., 124.
50. Ron Trudinger, *Cells for Life* (South Plainfield, NJ: Bridge Publishing, Inc., 1984), 34.
51. Elmer L. Towns, *An Inside Look at Ten of Today's Most Innovative Churches* (Ventura, CA: Regal Books, 1990), 44.
52. Ibid., 78-81.
53. Ron Trudinger, *Cells for Life* (South Plainfield, NJ: Bridge Publishing, Inc., 1984), 14.
54. Ibid., 17
55. Ibid., 112
56. Rodney J. Dean and Gary L. McIntosh, *How to Start or Evaluate a Small Group Ministry* (Lynchburg, VA: Church Growth Institute, 1991).
57. Ibid., 48-49.

DATE DUE

Demco, Inc. 38-293